Hudson River Panorama

EXCELSIOR EDITIONS, AN IMPRINT OF STATE UNIVERSITY OF NEW YORK PRESS *and* ALBANY INSTITUTE OF HISTORY & ART

HUDSON RIVER PANORAMA

A Passage through Time

Tammis K. Groft, W. Douglas McCombs, Ruth Greene-McNally

With a Foreword by Christine M. Miles and an Essay by John R. Stilgoe photography by GARY GOLD, JOSEPH LEVY, *and* MICHAEL FREDERICKS

custom digital image preparations by ALLISON MUNSELL

Published by
STATE UNIVERSITY OF NEW YORK PRESS, ALBANY

© 2009 Albany Institute of History & Art

Printed in the United States of America

Excelsior Editions is an imprint of State University of New York Press.

For information, contact
State University of New York Press, Albany, NY
www.sunypress.edu

Production and book design, Laurie Searl
Marketing, Fran Keneston

LIBRARY OF CONGRESS CATALOGING-IN-PUBLICATION DATA

Groft, Tammis Kane.
Hudson River panorama : a passage through time /
Tammis K. Groft, W. Douglas McCombs, and Ruth Greene-McNally;
with a foreword by Christine M. Miles; and an essay by John R. Stilgoe.
p. cm.
Includes bibliographical references and index.
ISBN 978-1-4384-3256-4 (pbk. : alk. paper)
1. Hudson River Valley (N.Y. and N.J.)—History.
2. Hudson River Valley (N.Y. and N.J.)—Social life and customs.
3. Hudson River Valley (N.Y. and N.J.)—Description and travel.
I. McCombs, W. Douglas. II. Greene-McNally, Ruth.
III. Stilgoe, John R., 1949- IV. Title.
F127.H8G86 2009
974.7'3—dc22
2009037201

10 9 8 7 6 5 4 3 2 1

(*facing page*)

SCALE MODEL OF THE STEAMSHIP MARY POWELL

Forrest Van Loon Ryder (1897–ca.1980), Coxsackie, NY
Wood, paint, and plastic, 1967
Gift of Mr. and Mrs. S. Vint Van Derzee in honor of Norman S. Rice
Photography by Gary Gold

Contents

Foreword

The Albany Institute of History & Art (AIHA), founded in 1791, is one of the oldest museums in the United States. Its outstanding regional collections, documenting the art, history, and culture of the upper Hudson Valley, place the museum at the forefront for promoting the area's rich cultural heritage. This book, *Hudson River Panorama: A Passage through Time*, derived from a major exhibition planned, curated, and presented by AIHA in 2009 to commemorate the Hudson-Fulton-Champlain four-hundredth anniversary celebration.

Research and development for this project began in 2005 thanks to visionary support from the Equinox Foundation. Using a transdisciplinary perspective, the Albany Institute's talented staff and a team of distinguished science and humanities scholars undertook an exploration of the art, history, and culture of the Hudson Valley as seen through the eyes of people who have lived in or traveled through it over the past four centuries. This book shares new research and rarely seen materials drawn from the Albany Institute's collections, which we hope will elicit enthusiasm and encourage further study of the Hudson River, one of America's first frontiers and one that continues flowing, growing, and developing each day.

The Hudson River, of course, is much more than a waterway. Since it first carved its way through what is now New York State, the river has been a source of sustenance, protection, habitat, and community for millions of people, plants, and animals. In more recent times, it has facilitated trade, enabled industry, and functioned as a natural conduit transporting people, goods, and ideas along its course; it has also been a source of cultural significance and insight. The Hudson Valley's ever-changing demographics have mirrored the ebb and flow of the river itself, shifting with transformations and advancements in American society, economics, and politics.

John Stilgoe's provocative essay, "River Reach," sets the stage by commenting on our relationship with rivers today and delving into river lexicons that add meaning to that relationship over time.

In an effort to communicate the many facets of the Hudson's story in a meaningful way, this book is organized into four overarching themes. First, "Natural History and Environment" surveys the river's flora and fauna and charts the involvement and impact of human settlement and industry, along with the efforts to protect the river's environment and scenic beauty. Second, "Transportation" explores the Hudson River as a great highway and the various ways locals and visitors have traveled on it, across it, or along its verdant banks. Third, "Trade, Commerce, and Industry" examines the revolutionary role of the Hudson in the American and world marketplaces, one whose impact is still being experienced globally. Finally, "Culture and Symbol" showcases the wealth of creative inspiration and cultural symbolism that has originated along the river, both from ingenious writers, artists, architects, and educators as well as from the landscape itself.

Hudson River Panorama is the result of the support, effort, scholarship, and diligence of many individuals and donors. I would especially like to thank members of the project team: Tammis K. Groft, Deputy Director for Collections and Exhibitions; W. Douglas McCombs, Curator of History; Ruth Greene-McNally, Research Curator; Allison Munsell, Rights and Reproductions and Digitization Coordinator; Tom Nelson, Exhibition and Graphic Designer; Barbara Bertucio, Registrar; Rebecca Rich-Wulfmeyer, Chief Librarian; Erika Sanger, Director of Education; Kristen Gilbank, Education Program Manager; Barbara Collins, Education Program Coordinator; Steve Ricci, Public Relations and Marketing Manager; Scot Morehouse, Visitor Assistant; Lori Veshia, Business and Human Resources Manager; Courtney Troeger, Executive Assistant to the Director; Jeannie Garber Patz, Membership and Events Coordinator; Andrea Lomanto, Corporate and Board Giving Coordinator; Amy Morrison, Individual Giving Coordinator; Elizabeth Bechand, Museum Shop Manager; Rob Nilson, Director of Facility Operations; Joe Benassi, Buildings and Grounds; and Thea Slaughter, Security Officer.

Key to the research phase of this project, the comments and insights from the following humanities and science scholars helped guide our vision: Harvey Green, PhD, Northeastern University; Christopher Lindner, PhD, Bard College; Tom Lewis, PhD, Skidmore College; John R. Stilgoe, PhD, Harvard University; Jon Erickson, PhD, University of Vermont; Harvey K. Flad, PhD, Vassar College; Christopher A. Hawver, Albany Pine Bush Preserve Commission; Robert Henshaw, PhD, Hudson River Environmental Society; Erik Kiviat, PhD, Hudsonia Ltd.; Dan Miller, PhD, Hudson River National Estuarine Research Reserve; Roger Panetta, PhD, Fordham University; and Steven O. Wilson, Hudson River Environmental Society.

Other individuals provided valuable assistance in the research phase of this project: Matthew Bender IV, Phoebe Bender, Marie Burns, Barbara Casey, Tom Lake, Fred LeBrun, Jennifer Lemak, Ellen Leerburger, Margaret Linen, Stephen Linehan, Marcia Moss, Stuart Pattison, Patricia Perrella, Norman S. Rice, Matthew Shaughnessy, Noah Sheetz, Stephen Stanne, Michelle Stefanik, Ward Stone, Len Tantillo, and Peter Ten Eyck II.

In closing, I would like to thank the Equinox Foundation for their early and generous support, which acted as a catalyst for hundreds of donors. Their interest and investment has enabled the Albany Institute to tell the story of the Hudson River in a manner as momentous as the four-hundredth anniversary of its exploration. I would also like to thank Joan Davidson and Furthermore, a program of the J. M. Kaplan Fund, for their contributions which enabled the Institute to meet its publication goal.

Christine M. Miles
Director, Albany Institute of History & Art

Acknowledgments

The Albany Institute of History & Art wishes to thank the following for their support:

Leadership Support:
Equinox Foundation

Major Project Support:
William Randolph Hearst Foundation, New York State Council on the Arts, Institute of Museum and Library Services, MetLife Foundation, New York Council for the Humanities, New York State Department of Environmental Conservation/Hudson River Estuary Fund, Bank of America Foundation, Bender Family Foundation, Matthew Bender IV, Phoebe Powell Bender, Buchman Foundation, Members United Corporate Federal Credit Union, Teaching the Hudson Valley

Additional Project Support:
74 State, Albany Parking Authority, Assemblyman Robert Reilly Salary Fund, architecture+, Austin & Co., Inc., William and Carol Bevilacqua, Caryn Zeh Appraisals, LLC, Civil Service Employees Association, The Desmond Hotel and Conference Center, Furthermore: A Program of the J. M. Kaplan Fund, Mr. and Mrs. Michael Golden, Hampton Inn & Suites Albany—Downtown, Hudson-Fulton-Champlain Quadricentennial Commission, Hudson River Foundation, Hudson River Valley National Heritage Area and the National Park Service, Hudson River Valley National Heritage Area/Greenway and the National Park Service, Lower Hudson Conference of Historical Agencies and Museums, Edgar W. and June B. Martin Fund, Louise and Lawrence Marwill, Gordon Mowbray, New York State United Teachers, Lucille A. Herold Charitable Trust, Richard and Karen Nicholson, Ellen Picotte, Francis M. Pitts and Deborah E. Byers, Joseph P. and Joan P. Richardson, Rockwell Fund, Colleen M. Ryan and Eric Hoppel, Scarano Boat Building, Inc., Trudeau Architects, Whiteman Osterman & Hanna

Future400 Society:
Dr. and Mrs. John W. Abbuhl, John T. Battin, In Memory of Melvyn L. Behn, William and Allison Bennett, Bill Bouchard, Dr. and Mrs. Wesley H. Bradley, Bonnie and Paul V. Bruno, Charles and Charlotte Buchanan, Carol Bullard and Worth Gretter, Mr. and Mrs. Michael K. Burke, Charles E. and Eva S. Carlson, Prentiss and Frieda Carnell, Lawrence W. Chakrin, PhD, Rhea and Jim Clark, Donna Crisafulli and Richard Kuhnmunch, Mrs. Edward J. Crummey, Mr. and Mrs. Roger J. Cusick, Jean Daniels, John DeCelle, Kimmey C. Decker, John K. Desmond Jr., Barbey and Ned Dougherty, Jennifer A. Drautz, John R. Dunne, Tom and Lisa Evans, John and Barbara Flynn, Neil and Jane Golub, Jane Graham, Peter Harriott in memory of Mary Lou Harriot, Tim and Hellen Harris, Susan M. Haswell, Arthur D. and Janet S. Hengerer, Beatrice Herman, Fred and Donna Hershey, Helen Phelan Howe, Ted Jennings, Jocelyn R. Jerry, Frances and Robert Kamp, Teresa A. Kennedy, Ruth and Don Killoran, James Kraft, Robert and Mary LaFleur, Keith C. Lee, Robert and Doris Fischer Malesardi, Maggie Mancinelli-Cahill, Victoria Manes, Chuck and Barbara Manning, Harry and Frances McDonald, Judith McIlduff, Bill and Kate McLaughlin, Robert and Mary McLean, in memory of Helen O. Meacham Stephens, John and Marney Mesch, John J. and Christine Miles Kelliher, Leland and Virginia Miles, Magda and Gus Mininberg, Stephen and Mary Muller, William J. Nathan, John J. Nigro, Donna Nowak-Hughes and Paul Hughes, Lauren Payne and Robert Clancy, Bill and Susan Picotte, Vera and Richard Propp, Robert and Claire Ruslander, Andrea Schulz, Francis and Cynthia Serbent, Susan Siegel, Ethel R. Silverberg, Spencer and Patricia Standish, Norbert Stegemann, Robert P. Storch and Sarah M. Lord, Jeff and Jeannie Straussman, Bill and Stevi Swire, William A. Thomas, James and Maureen Tusty, Mr. and Mrs. Robert L. Ungerer, In Memory of Elliot J. Wachs, Thomas Whalen, Gary H. and Rebecca J. Wilson, Anonymous (4)

Albany from the East Side of the Hudson River

William Hart (1823–1894)
Oil on canvas, 1846. Gift of the Vosburgh Estate, x1940.636.2
Photography by Gary Gold

River Reach

Reached a river lately? Fetched home an understanding of some fragment of the riverine whole? Nowadays watching a river proves uncommon, and noticing a river grows rare. Most people glimpse, often guiltily as their eyes flick sideways from high bridges; they shiver as cars sway over lane markings and vertigo twitches steering wheels. Even back-road motorists drive too fast to observe. Little people see less. In booster seats and backseats, children peer at guard rails paralleling highways paralleling rivers; corrugated steel ribbons block views of adjacent scrubby vegetation camouflaging the water beyond. Train passengers peering out at parallel water speed too rapidly to orient themselves in relation to flowing water, seeking only landmarks to reassure themselves of schedules kept. Adults determined to reach a river, to get out onto its water, to get a sense of it and its environs, find access intricate, often difficult, and frequently impossible. If anything, American rivers become obstacles, vaguely perceived barriers necessitating driving to the next bridge. Traffic flow makes them wraiths flowing and curving beyond and often beneath notice. Elites may enjoy riverbank views before they cloy and boaters may course a few miles upriver or down, but the bulk of Americans realize rivers indirectly and weakly. And what they see they often cannot name and indeed may see vaguely, because riverine toponymy has all but vanished. What cannot be designated often flows past unremarked and unnoticed.

Americans realize less of rivers now than they did even five years ago. Computer-generated driving directions and in-car navigation systems deflect attention from highway maps and road atlases. A fundamental perceptual change that arrived stealthily and unmentioned by high-tech aficionados skews riverine knowing in ways signaling a dramatic shift in American culture. Ten years ago highway maps delineated rivers, indicating if nothing else where motorists might expect bridges and why. Only recently have rivers begun to disappear from maps, perhaps because frantic drivers try turning from red-marked interstates onto what seem to be blue-line secondary or tertiary roads. Noticing the important that is not there, remarking what has gone missing in everyday life, remains one of the hardest of life skills to master. But nowadays observers of ordinary American behavior descry few drivers pulled onto the shoulder and studying maps. Motorists swerve into gas stations and fast-food restaurants or pause on the side of the road to make cell phone conversation, not to unfold a map and judge where best to negotiate a river crossing. No longer do rivers reach road maps. On-board navigation systems indicate little about pleasant river views or locations where prime property might be had cheaply. Often they indicate nothing of rivers.

Rivers and maps drift into a national perceptual gore. When highway construction or collision deflects motorists onto alternate routes unmentioned in printed-out directions and absent from dashboard navigational devices, drivers scrabble for old maps. If they find them buried in the unconsciousness of glove compartments or trunks, they have a chance to locate themselves in terms of personal intention and geography both. That chance, especially if the map is old, holds the possibility of perceiving a river in larger frames. But all too often, the alternate-route driver discovers a river accidentally, and, confronting the decision to turn upstream or down in search of a bridge, stops to ask for direction. Sometimes the verbal directions prove useful. Often they do not. Many people who live and work in the purlieus of rivers know little of the flow shaping the larger landscape fabric. Only rarely do the lost and the newcomers hear any of the old terminology that designates what rewards scrutiny.

Direct physical contact with rivers often involves post-parking inconvenience, the down-slope scramble into poison ivy and sumac nuzzling guardrails, rocks and mud, then precarious footing along-side moving water of uncertain depth. Adjacent to cities and small towns, nestled against well-maintained railroads and highways, a ribbon of wilderness separates ordered space from flowing water.

Vegetation blocks short-distance views. From just above, even from the height civil engineers determine is safe from hundred-year flooding, the surface of the water seems near and very often inviting. A few steps into the undergrowth means always a few feet ratcheting down a slope that often startles and sometimes terrifies. Rotting leaves and grass slide atop mud and gravel, causing explorers to grab tree trunks and branches, even poison ivy vines; descent makes intent precarious and sometimes reverses it. Half scrambling, half falling, explorers fear for good clothes, dry shoes, and their own safety. Often vegetation ends in sunlight, open views, and sheer drops which trick even overconfident dogs.

Then views baffle. From the edge of the river, only water composes the foreground and middle distance, unless a floating log drifts past or a pleasure boat or barge zips or chugs along. Distance wrecks most notions of scale. Rivers seemingly knowable and casually manageable from afar become vast, almost grossly fearsome up close. Unlike lakes, their water moves. Riverside vegetation, however unpleasant and prickly, lingers behind the modern viewer as a potential project for access-ramp professionals, but the subtle snakelike force of great rivers defies human effort. Direct contact with rivers shrinks the contemporary American confidence born in cul-de-sacs and shopping malls; intimacy with great rivers shrivels it. Current fixes attention, then molds it, often drawing smugness and arrogance from observers so close they might become part of the river, absorbed by it, carried away.

Parents tell children to be careful of the slithering power. They grab the hands of toddlers and order obstreperous youngsters to be quiet. Except in rapids, the current moves silently, and adults sense the appropriateness of low-voiced, sustained attention in the face of implacable force. Unlike thunderstorms and even high winds, the current makes no noise and indeed is scarcely discernible to the eye. It is dangerous in its muteness.

At first the current drains the spirit. It makes the psyche tributary, pulling from it the casual modern understanding of geomorphology, genuine landscape, actual natural system. Intimate encounter with a great river unnerves and humbles, and many people turn away quickly, scrabbling uphill through the scrub to the safety of roads, cars, and built landscape away from the streaming force. But a longer encounter opens portals of knowing through which the current flows. However slippery the riverine shore, it is the margin of another way of knowing, the zone marking hyper-real from virtual environment.

Physically reaching a river typically proves inconvenient. Reaching a river intellectually proves equally awkward at first but rewards those who explore beyond contemporary obliviousness and the fascination of virtual reality. In time, explorers reach reaches and begin to realize.

Lexicographers define *reach* more simply than river navigators used the term centuries ago. In his 1769 *Universal Dictionary of the Marine*, Englishman William Falconer explained a reach as "the line, or distance, comprehended between any two points on the banks of a river, wherein the current flows in a straight uninterrupted course." Noah Webster used the definition almost verbatim in his 1828 *American Dictionary*, but thirty-one years later in his *Dictionary of the English Language*, Joseph E. Worcester, Webster's chief American competitor, added a second definition: "a low piece of land or rock extending into the water, as on the sea-coast." Only at the close of the nineteenth century, when the Century Company briefly challenged the supremacy of Merriam-Webster lexicography, did a general dictionary encompass a bit of the subtlety river navigators casually accepted. "A continuous stretch or course, an uninterrupted line of extension or continuity: as a *reach* of level ground; an inland *reach* of the sea; a *reach* of a river (a straight course between bends); a *reach* of a canal (the part between locks, having a uniform level)," averred the *Century Dictionary* in 1891. In 1932, having reasserted its dominance in American word defining, Merriam-Webster published its *New International Dictionary*. It first offered a seemingly more complex definition of the term: "An extended portion of water or land; a straight portion of a stream or river; a level stretch, as between locks in a canal; an arm of the sea, extending up into the land; a promontory or tongue of land." But it linked that usage with another that it designated "nautical": "A leg or board sailed by a vessel between tacks; also, a course of sailing with the wind forward of the beam but not enough so to compel tacking. A reach is *close* when the vessel has to sail close to the wind; broad when the wind is almost abeam." Twelve years later, René de Kerchove's *International Marine Dictionary* distinguished not only between the topographical meaning and the nuances of sailing ("a sailing boat under way is said to be reaching when neither beating to windward nor running before the wind"), but also between "the straight course between the bends of a river" and "a straight part in a navigable river." Falconer and de Kerchove frame subtle but significant shifts in American perception of rivers, especially estuarine rivers.

In the same year that Henry Hudson sailed into the river now bearing his name, Philemon Holland published a translation of Ammianus Marcellinus's *Roman History*, shaping classical Latin terminology into then-modern English: "And now by this time augmented with snow, melted, and resolved into water, and racing as it goes among the high banks with their curving reaches, the river entereth into a deep and vast lake," Holland wrote of a Roman legion confronting dangers worse than Germanic barbarians. Period English proves important now, because much contemporary American riverine vocabulary has become once again the vocabulary of landsmen confronting rivers as obstacles.

In 1720 Daniel Defoe addressed this awkward subject in his *Memoirs of a Cavalier*, which he advertised as the true story of an English officer in the service of King Gustavus Adolphus in the Thirty Years' War a century earlier. "Having gained a little height, where the whole course of the river might be seen," the cavalier recalled, "the king examined every reach and turning of the river by his glass, but finding the river run a long and almost a straight course he could find no place he liked" as a place to move his army across. "But at last turning himself north and looking down the stream, he found the river, stretching a long reach, doubles short upon itself, making a round and narrow point," and, after sending a disguised dragoon to sound the depths, moves his army across. Finding a ford or a safe place to ferry across troops figures in the whole settlement of North America, not only in "Washington Crossing the Delaware" and other painted vignettes. For the pioneer, the would-be settler, the trader,

and the pedestrian or equestrian traveler, a reach typically meant a slower, broader-based current than the rapid, twisting ones at bends, although often bends offered useful sandbanks. Americans tend to find what Arthur Young remarked in his 1792 *Travels in France*: governments build bridges at the location of ferries, and ferries tend to be located in the midst of reaches.

For the navigator, terminology necessarily meant something ever so slightly different, and in the long age of American river travel, roughly from contact until the railroad triumph in 1870, landsmen picked up fragments of riverine speech with every passage. When Holland published a translation of Pliny the Elder's *The Historie of the World* in 1601, he struggled with the classical description of the Ionian shore: "all the coast thereof is very full of creekes and reaches," Holland wrote, "the first gulfe or creeke appearing to the seafarer being named Basilicus." At the beginning of the twenty-first century, Americans in the northern part of the nation casually refer to shallow ocean inlets, especially those in saltmarsh, as "creeks," but they use *brook* to designate the small flowing streams southerners call "creeks." Dutch terminology lingers along the Hudson, where flowing freshwater remains a *kill* even when it becomes salty or at least regularly altered by the tides. Maine lobstermen unthinkingly accept the name "Eggmoggin Reach" and rarely ponder the rarity of *reach* in shoreline American nomenclature. And Hudson River navigators seldom think about the deep cultural and linguistic confusion implicit in the name "Crescent Reach," a length of river more apt to be vaguely perceived as separating Anthony's Nose and Fort Montgomery. Almost no one wonders if a reach is straight or curved. American lexicographers have long struggled with riverine terminology in large part because rivers vary, and one or two present significant awkwardness to lexicographers and thoughtful observers looking carefully at rivers and their artifacts.

The Hudson River is one of perhaps two fjords in lower North America, Saguenay Fjord in Quebec being the other. Geologists understand fjords as valleys eroded far below sea level by glaciers and filled by ocean water after glacial melting; unlike almost all rivers meeting the sea, fjords are deepest upstream of their mouths. At West Point, the Hudson runs 175 feet deep, although its depth varies with the tides. U.S. court decisions, recorded in multiple editions of Henry Campbell Black's *Law Dictionary* after 1891, emphasize that salinity has little to do with legal definitions of *tidal*. All that is necessary is that the water level move with a lunar periodicity related to that of the ocean at the mouth of a river. Even when defined by federal and state courts, water terminology remains sometimes regional (only in Louisiana can a lake have a current); riverine terminology always perplexes the unwary reader of period travel narratives and other documents. Worcester felt compelled to explain the correctness of *ostiary*, a term he rooted in the Latin *os* for mouth, but one now long abandoned for *estuary*, a word evolved from another Latin root, *aestuarium*, meaning the swell of the sea. By 1934 Merriam-Webster understood two meanings of *estuary*: where river current meets the tide and becomes more or less brackish, and where the combined flow moves with ocean waves.

Such distinction opens on longstanding local usage and national vagueness. In his 1848 *Dictionary of Americanisms*, John Russell Bartlett defined the Hudson River term *kill* as "a channel, or arm of the sea; a stream, river," noting that "this Dutch appellation is still preserved in several instances," among them Kill van Kull separating Staten Island from Bergen Neck. Webster had dismissed *kill* abruptly two decades earlier, calling it "a Dutch word, signifying a channel or bed of a river, and hence a stream," and Worcester did little better, calling it "a channel or watercourse; an arm of the sea." But a century later, Merriam-Webster explained it as rooted in the Old Norse *kill*, meaning a channel or inlet and still meaning such, although broadened to include creeks and streams and their vicinity, as in Peekskill and Catskill. The *New International Dictionary* directed readers to the second definition of *binnacle*, explaining that the word once meant not only a nautical compass but also a secondary or diverted channel; English usage had misspelled and combined the Dutch *binnen* (meaning "within") and *kill* but kept their meanings. A century later, lexicographers had ceased to define *binnacle* and other riverine terms still in regular use, especially along the Delaware, Mohawk, and Hudson rivers. Riverine terminology had become wraithed in river mists but survived like a Hudson River sturgeon, far in the depths of the American language.

Writing in a 1901 issue of *Dialect Notes*, Edward Fitch explained that *binnekill* remained in regular usage in New York from Kinderhook to Schenectady and especially in Delaware County, and that it meant something more specific than "a crooked creek." River people understood it to designate a secondary, typically shallow channel beginning at an eddy and sometimes rejoining the main channel of a river or stream. Fitch insisted that he had heard *vly* and *clove* used to further distinguish such secondary or tertiary channels, but by 1901 only a handful of lexicographers noticed such terms. The *Century Dictionary* defined *clove* as "a ravine or rocky fissure, a gorge: as the

Kaaterskill clove in the Catskill Mountains" and noted that Dutch words remained prominent "principally along the Hudson River in New York." It understood *vly* or *vlei* as perhaps a corrupted form of *valley* but decidedly Dutch in origin and designating a swamp or marshy pool, often dry in midsummer. Three decades later, Merriam-Webster understood it as an American term identifying swamps and marshes but in New York specifically designating a creek somehow different from a kill. The precipitous decline in passenger and freight river travel deflected the attention of well-educated Americans from the words that once made sense of river components, and today the terms linger in local usage and in period description. Like artifacts in a museum, they make the curious explore.

Nowadays even good dictionaries rarely define river terms. They present *clove* in a way that enables children to make no sense of cloves of garlic, cloven-hoofed livestock, and, perhaps especially for those anxious to boat along rivers, clove hitches. Lexicographers focus on the spice, not the variant adjectival meanings of *cleaved*, let alone on *vly* and its dialect relations to *vale* and *reach*. So many terms linger along rivers, especially along the Hudson. *Reach* stands obliquely related to *stretch*, but today the latter term proves more congenial to Americans enjoying a "pretty stretch" of road and utterly unmindful that reaching often involves stretching, and that a zig-zagging Hudson River sloop reached or "ratcheted" along the river. *Fetch* drifts at the level of dogs and sticks, and few Americans know it as a near synonym for *ghost*, an apparition that most certainly appears and sometimes takes the viewer, as a river sometimes takes those who fall into it. But river people know meanings of *fetch* now lost to landsmen.

Fetch designates "the extent of a bay or gulf from point to point" according to de Kerchove, who notes precisely that it also means "to make a desired point particularly when there is an adverse condition of wind or tide to be reckoned with. Also called to reach." Nowadays only long scrutiny makes clear the efforts of so many sailing vessels frozen in landscape paintings ostensibly about rivers, vessels reaching or ratcheting or fetching, vessels being fetched by wind or current or tide toward or away from reaches or points or into binnacles.

All the terms whisper but whisper rarely now. Hearing the whispers begins in seeing, noticing a river long enough to realize it, to think a bit about its shape and framework, and it begins too in noticing an artifact from the history of a river, something stranded in the flow of time. Noticing riverine artifacts closely enough to realize them, to wonder at their significances, is a way to move oneself into the flowing curve of time that courses everywhere rivers reach.

John R. Stilgoe
Orchard Professor in the History of Landscape at Harvard University

Introduction

When nineteenth-century historian and engraver Benson J. Lossing wrote *The Hudson from the Wilderness to the Sea*, first published in 1866, he opened with remarks on the significance of New York's Hudson River. "It is by far the most interesting river in America," he commented, "considering the beauty and magnificence of its scenery, its natural, political, and social history, the agricultural and mineral treasures of its vicinage, the commercial wealth hourly floating upon its bosom, and the relations of its geography and topography to some of the most important events in the history of the Western hemisphere."

The Albany Institute of History & Art (AIHA) has been a prominent part of the Hudson River valley for more than two hundred years. In 1791 a group of educated professionals, political leaders, and businessmen in New York City founded the Society for the Promotion of Agriculture, Arts, and Manufactures, the progenitor of today's Albany Institute. As an informal advisory board to the state legislature on matters concerning manufacturing, agricultural development, and internal improvements, the society moved to Albany in 1797 along with the state government, and in Albany, after several changes in name and purpose, the Albany Institute still resides, not far from the banks of the Hudson River. During its two hundred years in existence, AIHA has built an impressive collection of art and historical artifacts, as well as important holdings of manuscripts, broadsides, maps, and published works. These collections, a visible affirmation of Lossing's words, narrate the rich and multifaceted history presented in *Hudson River Panorama: A Passage through Time*.

That history began in September 1609, when Henry Hudson and his crew navigated their way up the Great River (now known as the Hudson) in search of the fabled inland passage to Asia. Although unaware of the long-term implications of his voyage, Hudson initiated a process of extraordinary transformation for life on and along the river. In the ensuing centuries, the Hudson River and its inhabitants have coexisted, at times peacefully, occasionally in uneasy association. The river has had an indelible effect on the region and its identity, yet its impact has stretched around the globe. *Hudson River Panorama* follows the river through selected stories organized into four themes:

NATURAL HISTORY AND ENVIRONMENT

A series of complex, interlinking ecosystems compose the natural environment of the Hudson River, a system that has been charted and studied for hundreds of years. Human settlement—first Native American and later European, African, and American—influenced and altered that environment. For more than a hundred years, Hudson Valley residents have led efforts to restore and preserve the river's natural beauty and habitats for future generations.

TRANSPORTATION

The Hudson River valley has functioned as a natural conduit, facilitating the movement of people, goods, and ideas. It has fueled transportation revolutions, including steam-powered boats, railroads, automobile highways, and airports, while canals have broadened the reach of the Hudson deep into the United States and Canada. For a system offering such opportunities for movement, the river has also been a barrier surmounted by ferries, bridges, and the forces of nature.

TRADE, COMMERCE, AND INDUSTRY

Consumer goods from around the world have flowed into the Hudson Valley on the river and along its banks. Products such as Chinese porcelain, Indian cotton cloth, and German automobiles create a cosmopolitan market. Trade and commercial interactions have also connected people, art, and design from diverse cultures. Filling distant markets with industrial and consumer products, Hudson Valley industries and farms bring economic benefit to the region.

CULTURE AND SYMBOL

Ideas, social movements, and cultural developments have originated along the Hudson River from writers, artists, architects, and educators inspired by the region's landscape and history. This rich storehouse of inspiration initiated a national school of art, a distinctive style of architecture and landscape design, and provided visual and cultural commodities for tourism. The Hudson has contributed to the formation of regional and national identities.

MODEL OF THE NEW YORK CENTRAL RAILROAD STEAM LOCOMOTIVE 999
Frank DeSantis (b. 1917)
Painted metal, glass, and wood, ca. 1940–1970
Gift of R. Paul Carey
1999.29
Photography by Gary Gold

NATURALISTS

First Descriptions and Misconceptions

When English explorer Henry Hudson sailed into the wide North American waterway he called the Great River (later named the Hudson River in his honor) in the autumn of 1609, he was working for the Dutch East India Company, searching for the elusive northern passage to Asia. For three weeks he explored the river until his ship, *De Halve Maen* (*The Half Moon*), arrived near the first set of waterfalls, a little ways north of present-day Albany. In a journal of the exploration, first mate Robert Juet described the valley as abundant with "great store of goodly Oakes, and Wal-nut trees, and Chest-nut trees, Ewe trees, and trees of sweet wood in great abundance."

In addition to these descriptions based on observation, seventeenth-century European mapmakers frequently illustrated their charts of the New World with exotic and mythical beasts, both on land and in the sea. In the absence of images drawn directly from nature, these depictions based on rumor and misinformation led to fanciful beliefs about the flora and fauna of North America.

WILD ANIMALS OF THE NEW NETHERLANDS
John E. Gavit (1817–1874), Albany
Original image from Arnoldus Montanus, *De Nieuwe en onbekende Weereld: of Beschryving van America* (Amsterdam, Netherlands, 1671)
Engraving on paper, ca. 1850
u1990.86

Mazell sculpsit.

A North West View of the Chohoes, or Great Cataract of the Mohawk River, in the Province of New York in North America.

The Perpendicular Height of the Fall 75 Feet. — Drawn on the Spot by Tho.s Davies Capt.t Lieut.t of the Royal Reg.t of Artillery.

First Views

Prior to the nineteenth century, most depictions of the American landscape followed the topographical tradition practiced mainly by British military engineers who received training in drafting and watercolor at the Royal Military Academy at Woolrich. Among them was Captain Thomas Davies, whose technical skills distinguished him as a military topographer and later as a central figure in North American landscape painting. Other British-born artists followed a different landscape tradition, the school of the picturesque promoted by English minister and travel writer William Gilpin. Perhaps the most prominent landscape artists working in the picturesque tradition in the Hudson Valley were the Scottish immigrant brothers Archibald and Alexander Robertson, who in 1792 founded the Columbian Academy, one of America's first art schools. Alexander produced several sketches of Hudson River landscapes while on a tour in 1796 and 1797.

In addition to landscape views, eighteenth-century military personnel produced detailed maps of the Hudson River valley; British captain John Montrésor's map includes well-rendered topographical details of hills and coastal harbors but also shows settlements and military outposts. Both British and American forces used his highly regarded map during the American Revolution.

A NORTH WEST VIEW OF THE COHOES, OR GREAT CATARACT OF THE MOHAWK RIVER IN THE PROVINCE OF NEW YORK IN NORTH AMERICA

Drawn by Thomas Davies (ca. 1737–1812)
Engraved by Peter Mazell (fl. 1764–1797)
Colored engraving, ca. 1768
1945.30
Photography by Gary Gold

Naturalists from Home and Abroad

The rich plant and animal life of the Hudson River valley and its impressive geological formations attracted the attention of American and European naturalists and scientists by the late eighteenth century. The detailed surveys, studies, and illustrations they produced recorded environmental conditions and changes, all the while reflecting prevailing ideas about nature and scientific investigation.

In 1785 fifteen-year-old François André Michaux of Paris accompanied his father André Michaux, a French diplomat and botanist, on an exploration of North American forests. François André returned to America in 1802 to collect and document tree specimens for the restoration of forests in France after the French Revolution. His associates, the botanical artists Pancrace Bessa and Pierre-Joseph Redouté, illustrated his *North American Sylva,* first published in Paris in 1817. Many of the species depicted grew in the Hudson River valley.

A fellow Frenchman, geographer and engineer Jacques-Gérard Milbert toured the Hudson Valley in 1815, similarly to collect plant and natural history specimens for the French consul general. Milbert also made drawings of most of the places he visited along the Hudson River. Upon his return to Paris, the drawings were published as the *Itinéraire Pittoresque du Fleuve Hudson,* which comprised fifty-three views. These prints form one of the most comprehensive and accurate depictions of the American Northeast in the period. They are also early examples of the relatively new medium of lithography.

In 1818 New York botanist and geologist Amos Eaton published one of the earliest works on geology in America, *An Index to the Geology of the Northern States.* Six years later, he helped co-found the Rensselaer School in Troy (later Rensselaer Polytechnic Institute). One of Eaton's students, Ebenezer Emmons, also a geologist and medical doctor, charted the geological composition of the Hudson Valley and surrounding regions in 1824, while another student, John Torry, published *Flora of the State of New York* in 1843 as part of the state-wide natural-history surveys that began in 1836.

Artists as Naturalists

During the nineteenth century, the mass-produced images found in books and as prints frequently romanticized the American landscape. Although many landscape painters produced formulaic or stylized compositions, several Hudson Valley artists made sketches directly from nature. William Hart, a second-generation Hudson River school painter, advocated for the expression of sentiment in addition to accurate composition in a series of lectures he prepared for the National Academy of Design. "Nature," he said, should "allow your picture to tell you what you feel."

Engraver John William Hill began his career as a city topographer and later focused on natural landscapes, mostly along the Hudson River valley. The artist Edwin Whitefield also produced a series of topographical town views that included Albany and Troy; in addition, he designed botanical studies for Emma Embury's book *American Wildflowers in their Native Haunts* (1845). Several of the plants depicted were found in the Hudson Valley. These various types of images helped to interpret the region's natural history and demonstrated the interconnection between scientific observation and artistic vision in the nineteenth century.

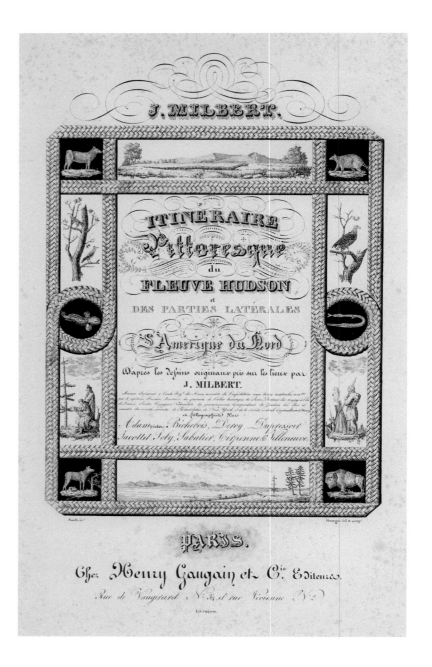

LITTLE FALLS AT LUZERNE.

N.º 1 of the Hudson River Port Folio

Published by Henry I. Megarey New York and transferred to G. & C.& H. Carvill New York.

Citizen Naturalists

In the collection rooms of natural history museums, slim drawers store neat rows of rare minerals, birds' eggs, and specimen insects. Amateur naturalists in the Hudson Valley compiled several of these once-common collections. Because most nineteenth-century naturalists were untrained, the term *amateur* held more status at the time than it does today.

Nowadays, the term *naturalist* signifies anyone engaged in preserving and understanding the environment. Numerous advocacy groups and public programs offer opportunities for inquisitive volunteers and interns who wish to contribute their time, experience, and observations. Active participation increases awareness of the regional environment and contributes observations that will serve as benchmarks in future centuries.

BROOK-LIME—DISTANT VIEW OF ALBANY

Drawn by Edwin Whitefield (1816–1892)
From Emma Embury, *American Wildflowers in their Native Haunts*
Printed by Lewis & Brown, New York City
Published by D. Appleton & Co., New York City
Colored lithograph on paper, 1845
u1990.067

PROVINCES OF NEW YORK AND NEW JERSEY (DETAIL)

Drawn by Capt. Samuel J. Holland
Published by Thomas Jeffreys, London, England
Engraving on paper, 1776
Map collection

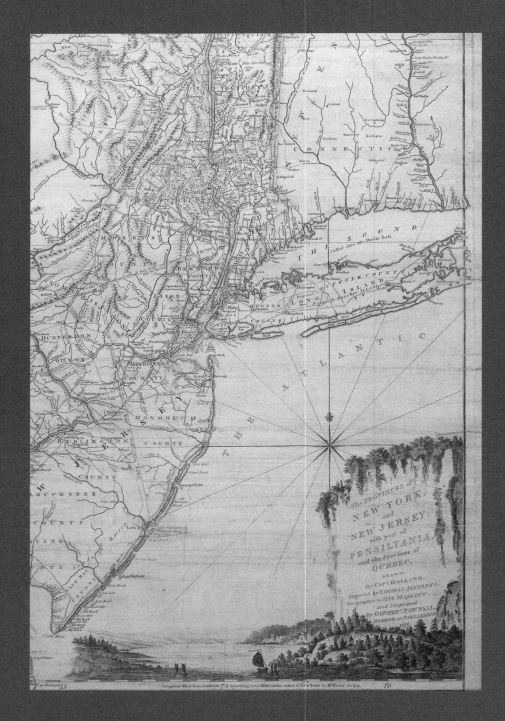

Pl.6

E.Emmon's del.   Bufford's Lith.N.Y.

DISTANT VIEW OF Mt MARCY.

EXPLORING THE SOURCE OF THE HUDSON RIVER

Charting the Course

The vast tract of land comprising much of northern New York was virtually unexplored and unsettled by Europeans and American colonists until after the American Revolution. The 1776 map of Captain Samuel Holland, British surveyor general for the Northern District of America, identifies the region as "Coughsaghrage, or the Beaver Hunting Country of the Confederate Indians." His map makes note that "This country is not only uninhabited but even Unknown except towards the south." Of great surprise, however, is a small lake depicted west of Lake Champlain that appears as the source of the Hudson River. Since no European or American had yet climbed Mount Marcy when the map was published, the alleged source was only conjectural.

Drawn by Verplanck Colvin

Lith. by Weed, Parsons & Co

LAKE TEAR OF THE CLOUDS.
The Source of the Hudson River.

Lake Tear of the Clouds

Drawn by Verplanck Colvin (1847–1920), Frontispiece from Verplanck Colvin,
Report on the Progress of the Topographical Survey of the Adirondack Region of New York
Published by Weed, Parson, & Co., Albany
Lithograph on paper, 1880. Library collection

The Adirondacks

In 1836 New York passed legislation to undertake a comprehensive survey of the state's natural history, including its fauna, botany, agriculture, and geology. Scientist and college professor Ebenezer Emmons oversaw the geological surveys in northern New York. His sketches of the mountainous terrain he encountered during the surveys first appeared in 1837 in "New York State Assembly Document No. 200." The views, lithographed by John Henry Bufford, depict some of the earliest images of the Adirondack Mountains and are the first instance of the use of the name "Adirondack" to identify the region. Several of Bufford's lithographs portray the High Peaks region, including Mount Marcy and Lake Colden. At the time of the survey, scientists and explorers believed this region contained the source of the Hudson River, although it took another thirty-five years to locate the actual origin.

Latitude N44.1067, Longitude W−73.9351

By the 1870s, scientists and surveyors involved with locating the source of the Hudson River came to an understanding that it should be the highest tributary that mattered, not necessarily the longest. After ascending Mount Marcy in the Adirondack Mountains in 1872, Verplanck Colvin, a topographical engineer from Albany and superintendent of the state commission for the Adirondack Survey, located a small pond at latitude N44.1067, longitude W−73.9351, which he named Lake Tear of the Clouds and identified as the source of the Hudson River. Colvin's selection, however, stirred controversy. Other contenders for the source included Round Pond, Lake Avalanche, and Lake Colden. Though opinions were divided over which lake was truly the highest, Verplanck Colvin described Lake Tear of the Clouds with such eloquence in his 1872 report—"a lonely pool, shivering in the breezes of the mountains"—that New York State legislators officially decided to designate it the source of the Hudson despite the controversy. With its surface at 4,293 feet above sea level, Lake Tear of the Clouds remains the official source of the river.

ENVIRONMENTAL CONSCIOUSNESS

Recording the Environment

Observing and recording the natural world have been fundamental activities in the Hudson Valley for centuries, even before the arrival of Europeans. Weather especially has been keenly watched, since it can affect farming, crop production, travel, and commercial shipping. During the eighteenth and nineteenth centuries, the printed almanac provided one of the most common guides for forecasting weather, while Hudson Valley residents and tourists have left behind plentiful accounts of meteorological occurrences. Yet the systematic recording of weather conditions has been left to amateur and professional scientists, individuals such as Albany physician Jonathan Eights and learned organizations such as the Society for the Promotion of Agriculture, Arts, and Manufactures, a direct predecessor of the Albany Institute of History & Art.

Several important devices for monitoring environmental conditions were developed and manufactured in the Hudson Valley. New York State Surveyor Simeon DeWitt proposed a design for a rain gauge in the early 1800s, and throughout the middle years of

AN
Astronomical Diary;
OR,
ALMANACK,
FOR THE YEAR OF OUR LORD
1 7 8 4;
BEING BESSEXTILE, OR LEAP-YEAR,
AND THE
Ninth Year of AMERICAN INDEPENDENCE.
CONTAINING,
The Motions of the SUN and MOON;
the Rising and Setting of the Sun; and the
Rising, Setting and Southing of the Moon.
ALSO,
The Eclipses—Judgment of the Weather—Length of
Days and Nights—Rising, Setting and Southing of
the principal fix'd Stars—Sun's Declination—Moon's
greatest North and South Latitude—Observable Days
of the Church—Tide, Interest and Expence Tables—
—a List of Roads to most of the principal Places
on the Continent: And the whole interspersed with
useful and entertaining Stories, both in Prose and
Verse.

Calculated for the MERIDIAN OF ALBANY.

BY NED FORESIGHT, GENT.

ALBANY:
Printed and Sold by S. BALENTINE, at his Printing-
Office near the Market-House.
☞ Great Allowance to those who buy to sell again.

the century, brass founder and scientific-instrument maker Joel W. Andrews of Albany made thermometers and hygrometers. Andrews also fabricated instruments that he used to estimate the altitudes of Mount Equinox, near Manchester, Vermont, and Mount Washington, in New Hampshire's White Mountains.

Today, during an age of dramatic climate change, historical observations of natural occurrences and meteorological recordings are crucial documents, as they provide valuable information for scientists to learn how the environment has changed or remained the same over the centuries.

Preserving the Forests, Creating a Park

When Europeans first settled the Hudson River valley in the early seventeenth century, the vast forests of the region appeared to constitute an unlimited resource of timber. But the accelerated cutting of trees, especially along the upper Hudson River, led to barren landscapes, soil erosion, and ecological problems by the 1800s. In 1864 Vermont naturalist George Perkins Marsh published *Man and Nature*, a work that enlightened perceptions about humankind's impact on the environment. Marsh's book linked deforestation with groundwater depletion and ultimately a reduced water flow in streams and rivers.

Eight years after Marsh's book, the New York State Legislature hired the young Albany explorer Verplanck Colvin to lead a multiyear survey of the Adirondack region. Colvin saw firsthand the harmful effects of unregulated lumbering in the upper Hudson River watershed and understood Marsh's warnings. In the ensuing years, he and others advocated for protection of the Adirondacks. Their first success came on May 15, 1885, when the legislature approved the creation of the Adirondack Forest Preserve. Greater protection for the Adirondacks came in 1892. After Glens Falls photographer Seneca Ray Stoddard presented to state legislators an illuminated glass slide show featuring his Adirondack photographs, Governor Roswell P. Flower signed

NORTH ELBA (ADIRONDACK MOUNTAINS)
David D. Coughtry (b. 1953)
Oil on canvas, 1984
1985 Purchase Prize, Mohawk Hudson Regional Exhibition
1984.25
Photography by Joseph Levy

the Adirondack Park Bill, ensuring that property owned by the state would be "forever kept as wild forest lands."

The Adirondack Park today encompasses six million acres of land, nearly half of which belong to the state. It provides enjoyment and recreation for more than ten million visitors annually.

Saving the View

The enactment of land-protection legislation and the formation of wilderness-preservation organizations such as the Appalachian Mountain Club (1876) and the Sierra Club (1892) escalated in the United States during the last decades of the nineteenth century and early years of the twentieth. Most efforts centered around natural-resource conservation, although in the Hudson Valley the river's scenic beauty was also at stake. Quarrying activities along the cliffs of the Palisades, opposite upper Manhattan and Westchester County, elicited a movement to protect this natural landmark. In 1900 the states of New York and New Jersey created the Palisades Interstate Park Commission, tasked with preserving the scenery of the cliffs. Within ten years, the commission had acquired and protected thirteen miles of land along the Hudson River.

As quarrying companies moved from the Palisades to the Hudson Highlands following the creation of the Palisades Interstate Park, preservationists likewise turned their attention northward. The Hudson-Fulton Celebration of 1909 further heightened awareness of the highlands' scenery and numerous historic sites associated with the American Revolution, such as West Point and Washington's headquarters at Newburgh. After failed attempts to establish a park, the New York State Legislature voted in 1910 to ex-

THE PALISADES
OF THE HUDSON

tend the jurisdiction of the Palisades Interstate Park into the Hudson Highlands, which allowed for the creation of the Bear Mountain–Harriman State Park. Within a few years, the park attracted nearly one million visitors annually, many from New York City; today it comprises two separate parks.

Hudson Valley residents are still making difficult choices between economic growth and scenic preservation. When the St. Lawrence Cement Company proposed building a new factory in Greenport in 1999, close to the historic homes of Hudson River school painters Frederic Edwin Church and Thomas Cole, residents and preservationists nationwide lobbied to protect the view. In 2005 New York's Department of State ruled against the cement plant as being inconsistent with its coastal-zone-management guidelines.

Modern Environmentalism

The modern environmental movement in the Hudson River valley formed during the 1960s by combining the earlier interest in preserving scenery advocated by the Hudson River Conservation Society with a commitment to halting industrial pollution and protecting the threatened ecology of the river.

PALISADES OF THE HUDSON

New York Central Railroad poster
Leslie Ragan (1897–1972)
Photomechanical print on paper, ca. 1930
Gift of the New York Central Railroad
1959.130.167
Photography by Gary Gold

STORM KING ON THE HUDSON

Homer Dodge Martin (1836–1897)
Oil on canvas, 1862
Gift of the estate of Anna Vandenbergh, 1909.19.3
Photography by Joseph Levy

In 1962 Consolidated Edison proposed building a two-million-kilowatt hydroelectric plant at Storm King Mountain. The proposal brought quick opposition. Not only did it threaten to deface a natural and historic landmark, but the proposed intake system would also endanger spawning striped bass. In November 1963, author and historian Carl Carmer, along with Frances Reese, Robert Boyle, and others, formed Scenic Hudson, an organization created to oppose the power plant. Years of litigation, public protest, and media coverage finally ended in a 1980 settlement, in which Consolidated Edison gave land they had acquired for their hydroelectric project to the Palisades Interstate Park Commission and the town of Cornwall, New York.

Among the individuals who galvanized environmental consciousness in the Hudson Valley was folk musician Pete Seeger from Beacon, New York, who first voiced concern for the health of the Hudson River in his 1961 song that began, "Sailing up my dirty stream." Years later, in 1969, he and friends built the replica sloop *Clearwater* as a floating classroom to bring greater awareness of the need for clean rivers. Around the same time, the Hudson River Fishermen's Association began monitoring industrial polluters with a community-watch program and the post of "river keeper," established in 1972.

The health of the Hudson River will continue to be watched in the twenty-first century as the Beacon Institute and IBM work together to develop the River and Estuary Observatory Network (REON), a monitoring and forecasting system comprising high-tech sensors and robotics. The system will ensure the Hudson River's protection and vitality for future generations.

THERE AND GONE: THE EVER-CHANGING SHAPE OF THE RIVER

Disappearing Islands

As a result of the natural cycles of seasonal change, geological transformation, and the human activities of dredging, building docks and wharves, and constructing dams, some islands that once dotted the Hudson River have disappeared, especially near Albany and Troy. Van Rensselaer's Island, originally opposite Albany near the east bank of the river, once offered a prominent position for viewing the capital city. The island was the site of a ferry station before bridges spanned the river, and the northern half of the island contained a mixture of private residences and small factories built on land once belonging to the Vischer family. Van Rensselaer's Island disappeared, however, during the early twentieth century as the channel of water separating the island from the east bank was filled and the riverside excavated and dredged away.

Park Island, also known as Island Park, met a similar fate. This island, located near the west bank of the Hudson River about halfway between Albany and Troy, was known for its sport and recreational amenities. In 1865 the Albany County Agricultural Society held its annual fair on the island, and a year later railroad magnate Erastus Corning I built a racetrack there that was said to be one of the best in the northeast. Construction of a new clubhouse and baseball diamond enhanced the island in 1885, the same year the Albany Bicycle Club hosted its races on it. Neither the park nor the island survives today, both victims of waterfront development and the building of Interstate 787.

ISLAND PARK RACEWAY

Unidentified artist
Oil on canvas, ca. 1888
Gift of Dr. and Mrs. Roderic H. Blackburn
1977.64.1
Photography by Gary Gold

(this page) VIEW OF ALBANY AND RENSSELAER

Richard Haas (b. 1936)
Watercolor on paper, 1979
Gift of Eliot H. Lumbard, 1996.24, Photography by Gary Gold

(facing page) CRYSTAL VALLEY FARMS,
A VIEW ON THE HUDSON RIVER AT THE OVERSLAUGH
William Croome (1790–1860)
Watercolor on paper, 1834
x1940.600.11, Photography by Gary Gold

Shaping the River

For centuries, human beings have shaped and altered the Hudson River to improve navigation, facilitate commerce and industry, and provide recreational and leisure amenities. Early maps and drawings of the river show a landscape somewhat different from the one we encounter today.

Some of the most notable changes occurred on the upper Hudson River between Albany and Coxsackie, where sandbars imperiled navigation. During the 1830s, longitudinal dikes, such as those south of Albany at the Overslaugh near Crystal Valley Farms, were constructed to confine the current and keep the main channel open. New York State approved a new series of dredging, dike repairing, and channel straightening projects in 1863; these were later taken over by the federal government.

Other changes shaped the river at Albany. In the early twentieth century, urban reformers proposed changes to the city's waterfront as part of citywide beautification efforts. On April 23, 1912, Mayor James B. McEwan requested that Albany architect Arnold Brunner "prepare studies for the improvement of the city," especially the area along the Hudson River. Much of this waterfront

belonged to commercial businesses and manufacturers. When Brunner declared that "the devastating ugliness of the old water front can no longer be endured," he voiced a rising opinion that the river's edge should serve the community and not merely the interests of individuals or corporations. In the end, only some of Brunner's recommendations were adopted.

The construction of Interstate 787 between Albany and Watervliet in the 1960s and 1970s, which led to straightening and smoothing of the Hudson's west bank, further altered the river's topography. Despite criticism, the project brought more than two hundred acres of riverfront land into public ownership through the creation of the Corning Preserve, which today offers recreational trails, boat launches, and protected wildlife habitat.

CULTIVATING THE HUDSON VALLEY

Early Cultivators

Archeological evidence reveals that the earliest cultivators of the Hudson River valley were Native Americans who raised indigenous crops, notably maize (corn), beans, and squash, along the banks of the river. Recent excavations on Pap-scan-ee Island, just south of Albany, have located the site of an early Mahican camp, originally

THE VAN BERGEN FARM
Attributed to John Heaton
(fl. 1730–1745)
Oil in board, ca. 1733
Courtesy of the Fenimore Art Museum

furnished with small bark houses, that was used for seasonal farming and fishing. Floral and faunal remains include raspberry and elderberry seeds, maize kernels and cob fragments, freshwater mussel shells, and bones of sturgeon and whitetail deer.

When Europeans arrived in the valley in the early seventeenth century, they brought new varieties of plants and animals as well as new methods of farming and cultivation. In 1678 the Dutch settler Marte Gerretse van Bergen bought thirty-five thousand acres of land near Catskill, New York, from Native Americans. Fifty years later, van Bergen's sons had established a prosperous farm located at the foot of the Catskill Mountains, depicted in

a rare painting from around 1733. This view shows a blacksmith shop on the right, Dutch-style houses in the center, and several hexagonal hay barracks with adjustable roofs for storage on the left. Horses, dairy cows, sheep, chickens, and dogs, along with a wagon filled with milk containers, figure in the image. In addition to members of the van Bergen family, four African slaves and two Native Americans complete the scene. Behind the farm, a fence separates the cultivated land from the wilderness beyond. The Swedish naturalist Peter Kalm made comments on cultivated lands and noted the abundance of apple trees, corn, wheat, rye, peas, potatoes, and grapes when he arrived in Albany in 1749. By

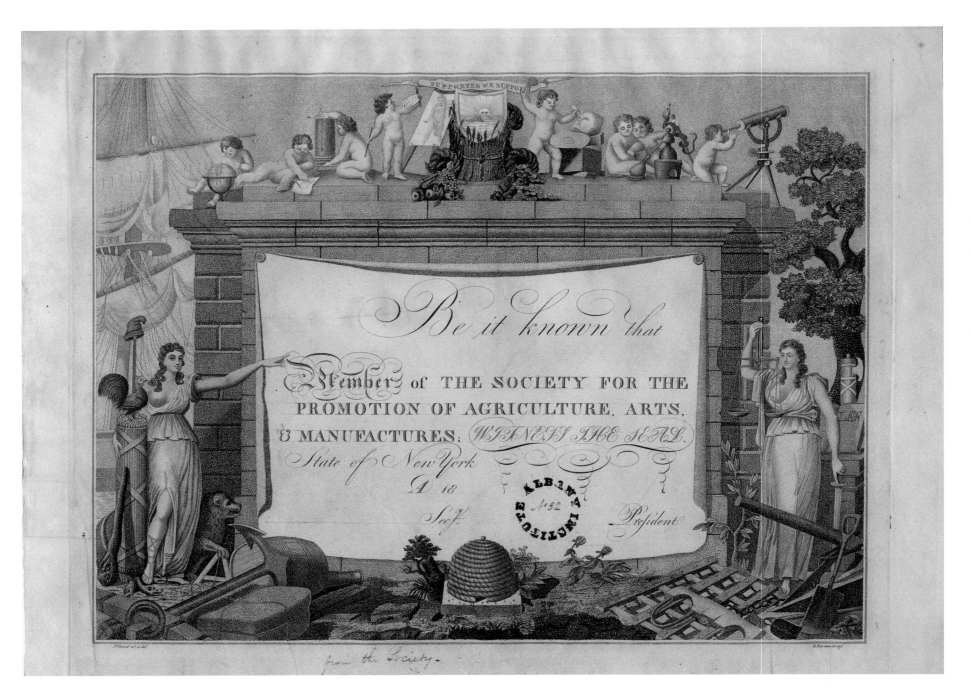

the middle of the eighteenth century, then, Hudson Valley farms generally resembled their European counterparts.

The Society for the Promotion of Agriculture, Arts, and Manufactures

Shortly after the founding of the United States, political leaders and men of learning began efforts to improve the nation's agricultural production. In New York State the first agricultural organization, the Society for the Promotion of Agriculture, Arts, and Manufactures (SPAAM)—the predecessor of the Albany Institute of History & Art—was formed in 1791 with the intended purpose of improving the state's economy and ensuring the welfare of its citizens through advances in agricultural methods.

In 1804 SPAAM was reincorporated as the Society for the Promotion of Useful Arts (SPUA). Papers written by members, including John Jay, George Clinton, and Simeon DeWitt, were published annually in *Transactions*. The society's first president, Chancellor Robert R. Livingston Jr., whose ancestral home of Clermont was located on the east bank of the Hudson River south of the town of Hudson, prepared several papers for the society, including an "Essay on Sheep" in 1807. Livingston specifically praised the merino breed for its high-quality wool. He imported breeding stock from France and soon established a flock of 145 sheep. Livingston advocated sheep breeding for the young nation in order to increase domestic wool production and decrease American dependence on imported European cloth.

The Society continued to emphasize agricultural achievements and began to offer prizes for the most useful discoveries and finest agricultural products, including the production of wool cloth that Livingston so actively promoted. In 1810 SPUA presented a silver bowl made by Albany silversmith Isaac Hutton to Samuel Bacon of Stillwater, Saratoga County, for the "Second Best Specimen of Woollen Cloth." SPUA's role in promoting agriculture eventually shifted to the New York State government, which established the Board of Agriculture in 1819.

Jesse Buel, Reformer and Educator

"To Improve the Soil and the Mind" was the motto promoted by Jesse Buel, one of New York State's most ardent advocates of agricultural improvement in the nineteenth century. A printer by trade and secretary of the New York State Board of Agriculture, Buel was well informed on the practical issues related to farming in this country and Europe, and he was determined to develop an agricultural college for educating farmers on the best scientific practices for improved principles of husbandry. He bought eighty-five acres of land in the Pine Barrens west of Albany, where he established his Albany Nursery. Using scientific methods—drainage, deep plowing, well-bred livestock, and manure for fertilizer—Buel transformed the sandy barrens into a veritable agricultural paradise.

In 1834, under the auspices of the New York State Board of Agriculture, Buel established *The Cultivator: A Monthly Journal Devoted to Agriculture, Horticulture, Floriculture and to Domestic and Rural Economy*.

A Sketch of the New York State Agricultural Society Fair, at Albany, 1850.

Drawn and printed on the Show Grounds.

LITH OF R. H. PEASE, IN THE TEMPLE OF FANCY, 516 BROADWAY, ALBANY. N.Y.

A SKETCH OF THE NEW YORK STATE AGRICULTURAL FAIR AT ALBANY

Drawn and Printed by Elisha Forbes and Richard H. Pease, Albany
Colored lithograph, 1850
u2005.13

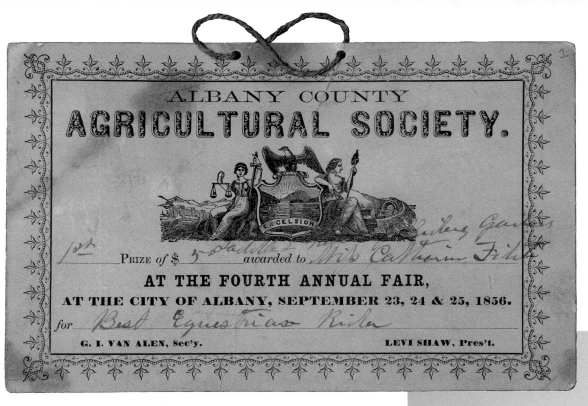

ALBANY COUNTY
AGRICULTURAL SOCIETY.

1st PRIZE of $ *5 Saddle &* awarded to *Miss Catherine Fitch*

AT THE FOURTH ANNUAL FAIR,
AT THE CITY OF ALBANY, SEPTEMBER 23, 24 & 25, 1856.

for *Best Equestrian Rider*

G. I. VAN ALEN, Sec'y.   LEVI SHAW, Pres't.

RED RIDING SHOES AND CERTIFICATE AWARDED TO MISS
CATHERINE FITCH FOR "BEST EQUESTRIAN RIDER" AT THE
ALBANY AGRICULTURAL SOCIETY FAIR

Wool felt and leather (shoes),
letterpress on pasteboard (certificate), 1856
Gift of Margaret Boom
1941.45
Photography by Gary Gold

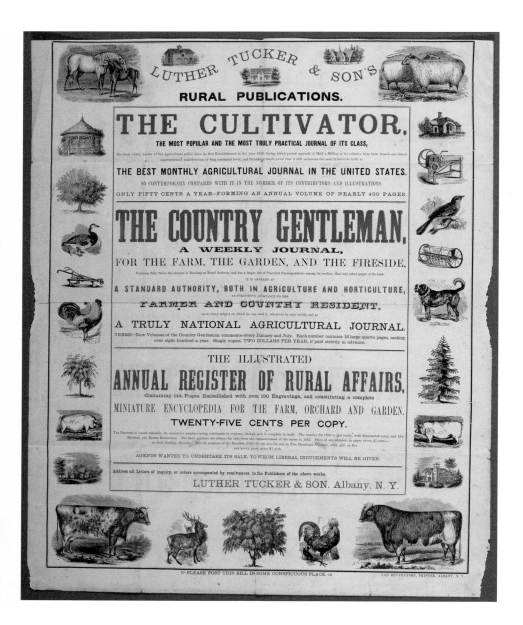

Published in Albany, it became the most popular farm journal in America. Illustrated articles addressed a variety of topics such as soil improvement, the management of bees, and how to skin a cow. In 1841 Buel's influence led the Board of Agriculture to appropriate money for the establishment of a state fair, which included a system for awarding prizes, a tradition that continues to this day. Throughout the second half of the nineteenth century, several manufacturers of agricultural equipment flourished in Albany, many receiving patents for improvements in time- and labor-saving tools and machinery, such as the Emery Brothers' plows and Charles La Dow's new and improved spading harrow.

Cattle on the Hoof and Canned Hams

Beginning in the 1850s, Albany became one of the largest wholesale cattle markets in the country, and cattle drives down Central Avenue were routine. Cattle were brought by train to the stockyards in West Albany for watering and feeding. From there they were reloaded onto trains bound for New York City and New England. Prior to the construction in 1866 of a railroad bridge across the Hudson River

BROADSIDE FOR THE CULTIVATOR

Proprietors Luther Tucker & Sons
Printed by Van Benthuysen, Albany
Letterpress and relief cuts on paper, 1860
Poster and broadside collection, PB 0265
Photography by Gary Gold

at Albany, cattle drivers forced cattle to swim across the river during summer months and walk over its frozen surface during winter.

With the advent of refrigerated railroad cars, Albany became a center for meatpacking companies, which employed large numbers of Irish and Italian immigrants. One of the best-known companies in the region, Albany Packing Company, later called Tobin Packing Company, processed First Prize products including ham, sausage, and lard until the 1980s.

Cultivating the Valley Today

Today in the Hudson Valley, farmers and agriculturists have taken a strong interest in artisan farming that emphasizes locally raised and made farm produce and products, such as cheese, honey, and wine, which are sold at local farmers' markets and through specialty suppliers and shops. Most of these growers rely on an influx of migrant workers from Mexico, Jamaica, and South America to harvest the crops during the months of July through October.

The Menands Market, established in 1933 by 530 farmers who banded together to sell locally and non-locally grown produce and

FIRST PRIZE HAM FINEST IN THE LAND, ADVERTISING POSTER
Albany Packing Co., Albany
Photomechanical print on cardboard, ca. 1940
1993.50.22
Photography by Gary Gold

flowers, is one of the oldest farmers' markets in the region. Louis Worthman, one of the founders, immigrated to the United States from Russia in 1910. The D. Brickman Wholesale Fruit and Produce Company, founded by Dave Brickman and his son Norman in 1945, has become a well-known vendor at the market.

In the upper Hudson Valley, the largest farmers' market occurs in Troy every Saturday. Established in 1999, the year-round Troy Waterfront Farmers' Market offers an array of goods grown and produced by more than fifty growers, bakers, chefs, and other artisans living within a one-hundred-mile radius of the city. Interest in producing and buying locally grown and made products supports a healthy regional food system and local economy.

BASKET OF TOMATOES, LOUIS WORTHMAN (1885–1979)

Harry Worthman (1909–1989)
Oil on canvas, ca. 1967
1993.31
Photography by Gary Gold

RIVER TRAVEL

Quiet Waters

For centuries before Henry Hudson's historic expedition in 1609, the Hudson River was a quiet passageway. Broad, undisturbed waters flowed between silent wooded banks. The passage of a solitary boat seemed an event, yet several Native American tribes used the river for travel and as a resource for food. When the first European explorers sailed into New York Harbor, they encountered native peoples, descendents of ancient civilizations living in migratory communities. These people were the river's first travelers.

Early accounts of Hudson's voyage describe hospitable natives approaching the European ship in twenty-eight dugout canoes filled with oysters and beans. The canoes were made from the light wood of the tulip tree, which grew abundantly on the banks of the river and as "large as three or four men standing together." To make the canoes, the Native Americans burned away the base of a standing tree, felled it with stone axes, and then hollowed out the trunk with fire and stone chisels. The Dutch called the tulip tree "canoe-wood" in reference to its ancient use among the native inhabitants.

PORTRAIT OF PAU DE WANDELAER (1713–AFTER 1763)
OR PAU GANSEVOORT (1725–1809)

Attributed to Pieter Vanderlyn (1687–1778), Oil on canvas, ca. 1730–1740
Gift of Catherine Gansevoort Lansing, x 1940.600.28
Photography by Joseph Levy

(*this page*)
THE STEAMER CLERMONT

Robert Havell (1793–1878)
Oil on canvas, 1840
1944.13. Photography by Gary Gold

(*facing page*)
R. B. WING & SONS, SHIP SUPPLIES

Unknown photographer
Albumen photographic print on card-
board mount, ca. 1870–1880
Manuscript collection, MG 16

Journeyed River

As European settlement of the Hudson Valley increased during the eighteenth and early nineteenth centuries, the Hudson River became a vital means of interchange between New York City and Albany. Various types of wind-powered vessels, including schooners, frigates, and sloops, sailed the river. These rigged ships facilitated trade, provided transportation, and defended the river and its communities from invading enemies. Despite their prominence, they moved unpredictably on the Hudson and were frequently stalled by unfavorable currents or shoals in its upper regions.

Travel on the Hudson River changed in 1807, when Robert Fulton set off on the maiden voyage of his steamboat *North River*. The voyage inaugurated the era of steam-powered transportation, a quick, reliable alternative to the vagaries of sail. Fulton established a steamboat monopoly on the Hudson that caused widespread opposition among sloop captains and independent steamboat operators. In 1824 Chief Justice John Marshall of the U.S. Supreme Court declared the monopoly unconstitutional, which opened the way for new steamboat companies and lowered the cost of fares from seven dollars for a one-way ticket to fifty cents. By 1865 boats traveling the river had advanced in design, with increased cargo capacity and better safety standards.

One hundred years after Robert Fulton's maiden voyage, railroads, the automobile, and airplanes eventually decreased travel on America's inland waterways.

Sports and Leisure

Hudson Valley residents commonly used rowboats as a means of travel on the river, but by the middle of the nineteenth century racing and competitive sporting events began, with established rowing clubs in Newburgh, Poughkeepsie, and Albany. Their well-publicized races attracted large crowds and extensive gambling among spectators, while cash prizes and trophies were awarded to the winning racers.

Winter weather and ice on the Hudson did not hinder sport and leisure activities. In 1790 the first iceboats used for transportation appeared on the frozen river, and the first ice yacht was built in 1861 in Poughkeepsie. These boats reached lengths of thirty to fifty feet and were transported between sites on rail cars. Ice sailing became popular at several locations on the Hudson River, where the sport continues today with active clubs. Depending on design and classification, today's iceboats reach speeds of sixty to one hundred miles per hour.

Current Travel

In the twenty-first century, the Hudson River continues to provide a means of convenient, economically viable, and scenic travel. Slow-speed barges transport commercial cargoes on the river, while sightseeing tour boats offer daily journeys to and from historic sites. Several clubs, businesses, and state parks offer opportunities for outrigger

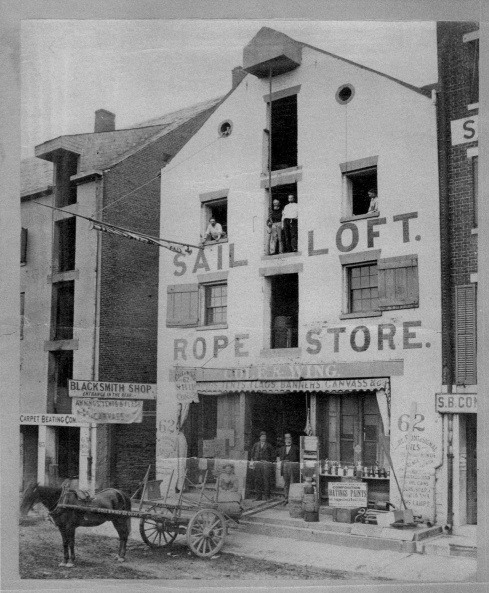

THE BEAVERWYCK CREW.

McDONALD, Phot., ALBANY, N. Y.

1876.

LOVING CUP PRESENTED TO THE BEAVERWYCK CREW
AT THE PHILADELPHIA CENTENNIAL EXPOSITION

Whiting Manufacturing Co., North Attleboro, MA
Silver, 1876
Gift of Mrs. William R. Hills, 1916.2.1. Photography by Joseph Levy

THE BEAVERWYCK CREW

Unidentified photographer
Albumen photographic print on cardboard mount, 1876
Photograph collection, series 17, no. 69

canoeing, rowing, sailing, rafting, and kayaking. Public awareness and improved river access have renewed interest in traditional small-craft boating for both residents and visitors to the Hudson Valley.

CANALS

Setting the Course

The concept for a canal linking the Hudson River to the interior of the North American continent originated in the eighteenth century. Following the American Revolution, the opening of land in the trans-Appalachian west created two needs: first, the need to survey and map western lands, and second, the need to build transportation infrastructure to bring western products to East Coast markets. In 1784 a young surveyor named Simeon DeWitt accepted the appointment of surveyor general for New York State, a position he held throughout his life. DeWitt surveyed much of the state by the late 1790s and began preparing a detailed map. The first edition of the map—measuring four feet by twelve feet—was published in 1802, while a smaller version appeared in 1804.

Prior to DeWitt's surveys, a group of private investors organized the Western Inland Lock Navigation Company in 1792 with the purpose of improving navigation along the Mohawk River for regional farmers. The joint-stock company accomplished little and constructed only two miles of canal by 1800, but it nevertheless stirred interest in a larger canal project.

In 1808 New York legislators set Simeon DeWitt to work surveying waterways between the Hudson River and Lake Erie specifically for the purpose of constructing a canal. Two years later, the legislature provided three thousand dollars for a board of canal commissioners (including DeWitt and his cousin DeWitt Clinton) to begin the task of building a canal. Construction officially started in 1817, with much of the labor performed by Irish immigrants.

Meeting of the Waters

A canal crossing New York State opened to great public acclaim in 1825, after eight years of construction. It was an engineering marvel. The Erie Canal spanned across New York for 363 miles, including 18 aqueducts and 83 locks that raised and lowered boats a total of 680 feet over its course between the Hudson River at Albany and Lake Erie at Buffalo.

Sections of the Erie Canal were already in use by 1823, when wheat from western farmlands reached New York City, but the official opening occurred two years later. Communities along the canal planned festivities, and a grand celebration took place in New York City in October that included fireworks, a parade, and parties. Governor DeWitt Clinton, one of the staunchest proponents of the canal, emptied a barrel of Lake Erie water into the Atlantic Ocean at Sandy Hook, a symbolic mingling of the waters. Furniture maker Duncan Phyfe produced small wood boxes from lumber cut in the Great Lakes and shipped to New York City via the canal. The boxes housed commemorative medals struck with the official seal of the Erie Canal, which depicted the classical gods Neptune and Pan to represent the Atlantic Ocean and Great Lakes.

Although traveling at only four miles per hour, mule- or horse-drawn canal boats opened towns throughout western New York to commercial growth, tourism, and immigration. Communities such

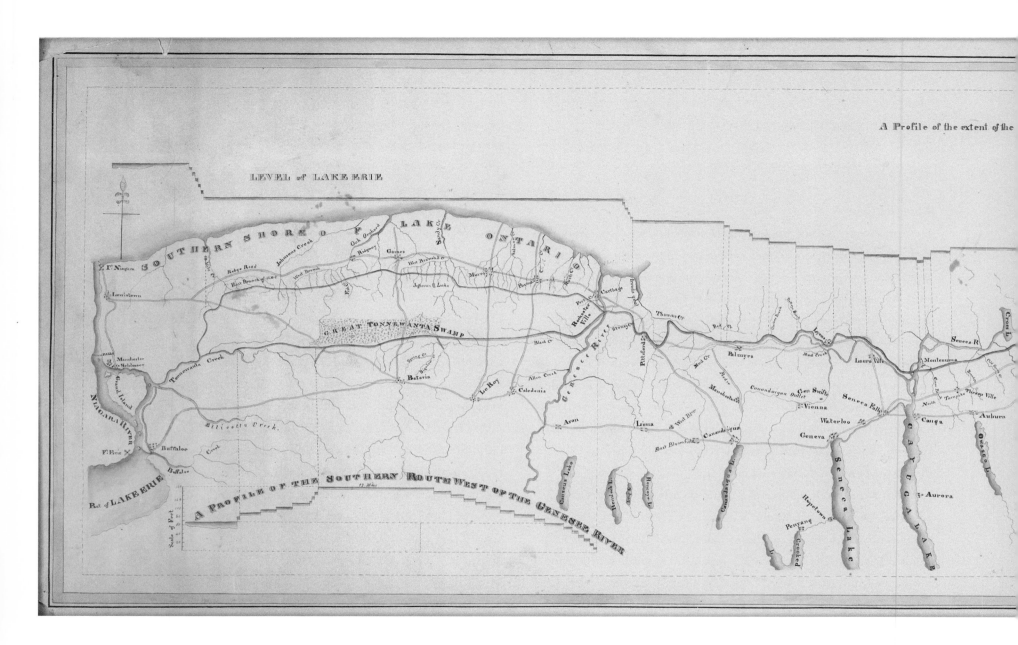

A Profile of the extent of the

LEVEL of LAKE ERIE

SOUTHERN SHORE OF LAKE ONTARIO

GREAT TONNEWANTA SWAMP

A PROFILE OF THE SOUTHERN ROUTE WEST OF THE GENESEE RIVER

Ft. Niagara
Lewistown
Manchester
Schlosser
Grand Island
Ft. Erie
Buffaloe
Port of LAKE ERIE
NIAGARA RIVER
Tonnewanta Creek
Elliotts Creek
Buffaloe Creek

Ridge Road
Johnsons Creek
West Branch
East Branch of N.M.C.
Oak Orchard
Ridgway
Gaines
West Branch Or
Jefferson Lake

Sandy Cr
Murray

Batavia
Spring Cr
Le Roy
Caledonia
Black Cr
Allen Creek
Avon
Lima
East Bloomfield

Genesee River
Stoney Cr
Pittsford
Rochester Ville
Carthage
Thomas Cr

Canesus Lake
Hemlock L.
Honeoye L.

Canandaigua L.
Palmyra
Manchester
Canandaigua Outlet
Gen Swift
Vienna
Canandaigua
Waterloo
Geneva

Mud Cr
Mud Cr
Lyons
Laura Ville
Seneca Falls
Seneca Lake
Hopetown
Penyang
Crooked L.

Montezuma
Seneca R
Cayuga
Aurora
Owasco L.
Auburn
CAYUGA LAKE

Scale of Feet
17 Miles

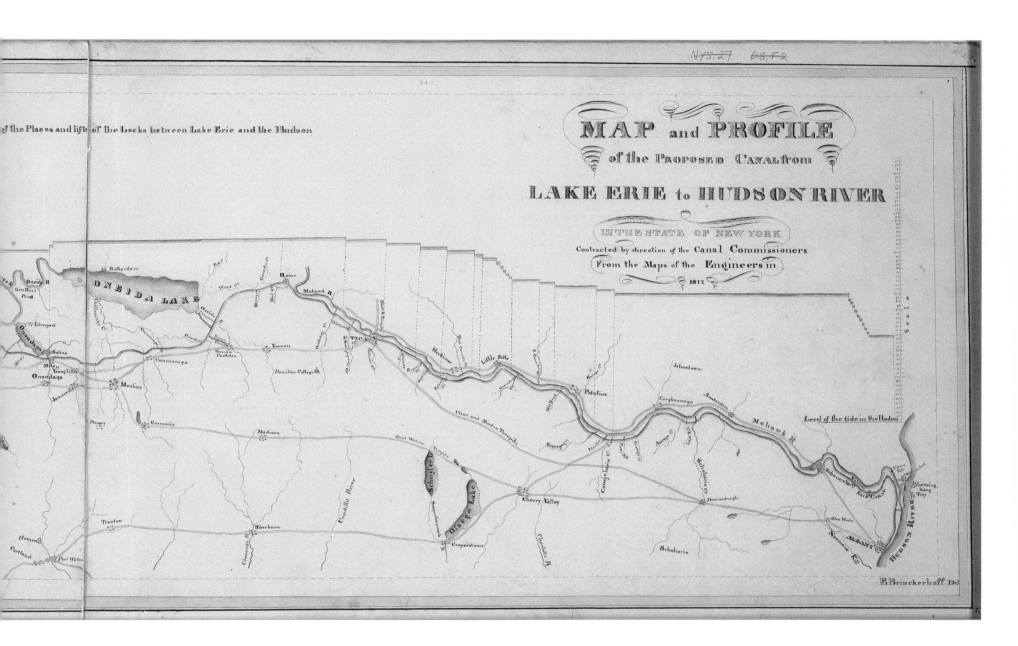

Hand-drawn map of proposed Erie Canal

E. Brinckerhoff

Ink and watercolor on paper mounted to linen, 1817

43

CONSTRUCTION OF THE ERIE CANAL

From Cadwallader D. Colden,
*Memoir Prepared at the Request of
a Committee of the Common Council of the City of New York*
Lithograph on paper, 1826
Library special collection

THIS BOX
was made out of a piece
of wood, brought from Erie
in the first Canal Boat
THE SENETA CHIEF

ERIE CANAL COMMEMORATIVE TOKEN
IN WOOD PRESENTATION BOX

Wood and metal with printed paper label, 1825
Gift of Albert B. Roberts
2006.49.10
Photography by Gary Gold

Little Falls. N.Y.
July 20th 1852. W. R. Miller. Del.

Herkimer C[?]

as Syracuse and Rochester thrived, while the falls at Niagara received thousands of tourists each year. The Erie Canal extended the reach of the Hudson River into the heart of the United States and connected interior communities with New York City and the world beyond America's shores.

The Erie Barge Canal

The Erie Canal prospered as a transportation system until the second half of the nineteenth century, when competition from railroads threatened the viability of the canal system. Several efforts to revitalize the canal and encourage more traffic were

undertaken, including the enlargement of canal channels and locks, completed in 1862, and the removal of tolls in 1882. But by the end of the century it became apparent that additional changes were needed, especially in order to accommodate larger barges with deeper drafts. The federal government considered funding a new expansion project but eventually backed out, leaving New York State to cover the entire expense.

Work began on the Erie Barge Canal in 1905 and finished ten years later at a cost of $140 million (about one-third the cost of the Panama Canal). The original Erie Canal had a bottom width of twenty feet and a depth of four feet; the new Barge Canal had a bottom width of seventy-five feet in the main channels and a depth of twelve feet. The project also included new locks and two reservoirs to provide an adequate water supply for the eastern section.

Unfortunately, the Barge Canal could not compete with railroads and the highway system of the post–World War II era. A 1928 article in the journal *Economic Geography* commented, "We have passed out of the canal and river period in transportation. Such waterways are obsolete in the United States." Today the Erie Barge Canal serves mainly pleasure boaters and tourists, and the 348-mile-long Canalway Trail opens the historic waterway to hikers, bicyclists, cross-country skiers, and sightseers as well.

BARGE PASSING THROUGH LOCKE 2, WATERFORD
Silver gelatin photographic print, ca. 1940
Postcard collection

ALBANY & BETHLEHEM TURNPIKE ROAD RATES OF TOLL
Unidentified maker
Paint on wood, ca. 1840
u1972.16.1
Photography by Gary Gold

PARALLEL TRANSPORT

Roads, Turnpikes, and Superhighways

The Hudson River has functioned as a natural highway for transporting goods, people, and ideas. Even the earliest roads took advantage of the level access along the riverbanks, as well as the access to hundreds of wharves that serviced cities, towns, and estates. Most early roads began as paths, which later became military roads, plank roads, and eventually paved or macadamized roads. By the late eighteenth century, turnpikes built by private companies charged tolls for people, wagons, sleighs, carriages, and all livestock. With the ever-increasing number of travelers from New York City to Albany and beyond, the demand for roads and services such as livery stables, stagecoaches, hotels, and restaurants expanded.

The development of the automobile in the early twentieth century led to the construction of bridges, tunnels, and highways such as the Taconic State Parkway, begun in 1924 and completed in 1963, and the Thomas E. Dewey Thruway, which opened in 1950. Like the early turnpikes, toll roads continue today, though travelers can now save time and money with devices such as E-ZPass.

ALBANY & BETHLEHEM TURNPIKE ROAD.
RATES OF TOLL.

FOR EVERY SCORE OF SHEEP OR HOGS,	6 Cents.
FOR EVERY SCORE OF CATTLE, HORSES OR MULES,	15 Cents.
{& So in proportion for a greater or less number of SHEEP, HOGS, CATTLE, HORSES OR MULES,}	
FOR EVERY SULKY CHAISE or CHAIR WITH ONE HORSE, 12½ Cents. N.B. {For this item, instead of the LEGAL TOLL the Company accepts,}	4 Cents.
FOR EVERY CART DRAWN BY ONE HORSE,	4 Cents
FOR EVERY CHARIOT, COACH, COACHEE or PHAETON, DRAWN BY TWO HORSES, 19 Cents, N.B {For this item, instead of the LEGAL TOLL, the Company accepts,} & Two Cents for every additional Horse,	12½ Cents.
FOR EVERY COVERED STAGE WAGON, DRAWN BY 2 HORSES, 12½ Cents. N.B. {For this item, instead the LEGAL TOLL, the Company accepts} and 2 cents for every additional Horse,	6 Cents,
FOR EVERY OTHER WAGON, DRAWN BY 2 HORSES, MULES OR OXEN, and 2 Cents for every additional Horse, Mule or Ox.	6 Cents.
FOR EVERY CART DRAWN BY 2 HORSES, MULES OR OXEN. and 2 Cents for every additional Horse, Mule or Ox.	6 Cents
FOR EVERY ONE HORSE WAGON DRAWN BY ONE HORSE.	5 Cents
FOR EVERY SLEIGH OR SLED, DRAWN BY 2 HORSES, MULES OR OXEN. and 2 Cent for each additional Horse, Mule or Ox.	6 Cents
FOR EVERY ONE HORSE SLEIGH,	4 Cents
FOR EVERY HORSE & RIDER,	4 Cents
FOR EVERY LED HORSE,	2 Cents

Railroads

On September 24, 1831, the first successful steam passenger-train to operate in the United States, the *DeWitt Clinton*, made its inaugural "grand excursion" from Albany to Schenectady in one hour and forty-five minutes. Its route eventually joined other lines to form the New York Central Railroad Company in 1853, guided by the business acumen of industrialist and railroad owner Erastus Corning I.

The New York Central Railroad, Hudson River Railroad, and the Delaware and Hudson Rail and Steamer lines were the premier rails servicing the Hudson River valley for more than one hundred years, until the mid-twentieth century. Not only did these lines guaran-

(*above*) VIEW ON THE HUDSON RIVER NEAR ATHENS, NEW YORK

George K. Nedtwick (1854– after 1912)
Oil on canvas, ca. 1890
1951.64
Photography by Gary Gold

(*right*) THE FIRST RAILROAD TRAIN ON THE MOHAWK AND HUDSON ROAD

Edward Lamson Henry (1841–1919)
Oil on canvas, 1892–1893
Gift of the Friends of the Institute through Catherine Gansevoort Lansing,
x1940.600.57
Photography by Joseph Levy

(*facing page*) NEW YORK CITY AND HUDSON RIVER RAILROAD advertisement

John S. Willard & Co., New York City
Lithograph on paper and reverse painting on glass in walnut frame, ca. 1880
Gift of the New York Central Railroad, 1959.130.9
Photography by Gary Gold

tee travelers speed and luxury, but they also transported industrial and commercial goods and employed thousands. The Pullman Company, the largest private employer of black labor in the United States by the 1920s, provided African Americans with stable jobs as waiters and porters on many train lines, including the New York Central. The New York Central Railroad also operated a large repair shop, known as the West Albany Shops, that employed hundreds of workers; eventually the site was replaced by a modern industrial park.

Some of the best-known trains running in the Hudson Valley included the *Empire State Express*, or the *999*, which set the world's land-speed record of 112½ miles per hour in 1893; the *Commodore Vanderbilt*,

THE *New* **20**TH **CENTURY LIMITED**

NEW YORK - *16 hours* - CHICAGO

NEW YORK CENTRAL SYSTEM

built in 1934; and the *20th Century Limited*. In 1971, faced with the collapse of passenger railroads, the United States created Amtrak (a portmanteau of *American* and *track*), a government owned and subsidized corporation designed to provide intercity passenger train service. Today passenger trains travel on the east side of the river and freight trains on the west.

The 20th Century Limited

The *20th Century Limited*, operated by the New York Central Railroad between 1902 and 1967, was the most celebrated passenger train in the nation during the twentieth century. Its route originated at Grand Central Station in New York City and terminated in Chicago, a run it could make in sixteen hours. In order to compete with

alternative forms of transportation, including the automobile and air travel, the New York Central commissioned industrial designer Henry Dreyfuss in 1938 to redesign the interior and exterior of the train to reflect the elegant, fashionable, and streamlined Art Deco styling of the period. Dreyfuss incorporated the New York Central's colors, blue and gray, and designed everything from the engine to the furniture, place settings, and matchbooks.

Air Travel

Albany played a significant role in the development of air transportation throughout the twentieth century. One of the first landmark events occurred just six years after the Wright brothers' first successful flight. In 1909, as part of the Hudson-Fulton celebration, publisher Joseph Pulitzer of the *New York World* offered a ten-thousand-dollar "World Prize" for the first sustained flight between New York City and Albany. The winner, aviator Glenn H. Curtiss, began his

(*facing page left*) THE NEW 20TH CENTURY LIMITED POSTER

From original painting by Leslie Ragan (1897–1972)
Lithograph by Latham Litho. Co., Long Island City, NY
Photomechanical print on paper, 1938
Gift of the New York Central Railroad, 1959.130.94
Photography by Joseph Levy

(*facing page right*) 20TH CENTURY LIMITED, END SECTION DINER

Henry Dreyfuss (1904–1972)
Gouache on paper, 1938
Gift of the New York Central Railroad, 1959.130.5
Photography by Gary Gold

THE ALBANY FLYER FLOWN BY GLENN H. CURTISS IN 1910 (DETAIL)

Unidentified photographer
Silver gelatin photographic print, 1910
Photography collection, series 17, no. 81

flight in Albany in a biplane he called the *Albany Flyer*, and after two hours and fifty-one minutes of flying time (not including two refueling stops), Curtiss arrived in New York City.

While the first landing strip in Albany lay several miles inland from the river, the second was on Westerlo Island, just south of the city (now the Port of Albany). Many early aviators, including Charles Lindbergh and Amelia Earhart, landed in Albany at one of these early fields. In 1928 Albany again made aviation history, when Mayor John Boyd Thatcher II purchased land for the site of the current airport from the Watervliet Shakers, creating America's first municipal airport. Airfare from Albany to New York City that year started at $25 and later dropped to $14.70. By 1930 Albany was the "aerial crossroads" of the Northeast. Albany's airport has changed and expanded many times since its opening, most recently in 1993 with a $184 million renovation project that resulted in a new name, the Albany International Airport.

The Underground Railroad

The Hudson River valley, with its network of roadways, railroads, and canals—and strong support of the abolitionist cause—became a successful avenue for the Underground Railroad, the secret organization that helped escaped slaves reach freedom in upstate New York and Canada. Key stations included Philadelphia, New York City, Albany, Troy, and Rochester. Stephen Myers, Albany's leading abolitionist, played an important role in the Underground Railroad. Born a slave in Rensselaer County, Myers used his skills as an eloquent public speaker, organizer, lobbyist, and journalist for the anti-slavery cause. He was associated with at least two aboli-

tionist newspapers published in Albany in the 1840s, the *Northern Star* and the *Freeman's Advocate*. Myers and his wife Harriet worked closely with other leading abolitionists and former slaves, including Harriet Tubman, Sojourner Truth, Frederick Douglass, and Dr. William Henry Johnson, who moved to Albany in 1851 and spent years advocating for the abolition of slavery.

Harriet Beecher Stowe's popular novel *Uncle Tom's Cabin* (1852) and its subsequent theatrical productions exposed the cruelty of slavery. Artist John Rogers, who was best known for making plaster sculptures highlighting themes from literature and everyday life, created works dealing with the issue of slavery such as *The Slave Auction*, sculpted in 1859. In another work, *The Fugitive's Story*, Rogers included the well-known abolitionists John Greenleaf Whittier, poet; William Lloyd Garrison, newspaper editor; and Henry Ward Beecher, minister and writer.

(facing page left) Photograph of Rosanna Vosburgh, former Albany slave who gained her freedom in 1820

Wood's Gem Gallery, Albany
Tintype, December 22, 1871
Thomas W. Olcott Papers, CS 550

(facing page right) God save the Union! Emancipation Convention Broadside

Letterpress on paper, 1863
Poster and broadside collection, PB0120

God save the Union!

The Friends of Freedom in Albany County will hold a Mass

CONVENTION!

IN THE CITY OF ALBANY,

On the 5th day of January, 1863,

TO RECEIVE AND TO RATIFY THE PRESIDENT'S EMANCIPATION PROC-
LAMATION, FREEING ALL THE SLAVES IN THE REBELLIOUS STATES, FOREVER.

God bless Abraham Lincoln, President of these United States.

On the 1st of January 1863, a new era in our country's history will be inaugurated. Then we
will rejoice and give thanks, and the praise to God, for the millenium is at hand. A Moses is found
who will lead the Children of Africa, out of American bondage; hereafter men shall not be enslaved,
neither shall nations, but both shall be forever free.

The Convention will Convene at 1 o'clock P. M., in the Methodist
Church, Hamilton Street, East of Lark.

The Friends of freedom in TROY, HUDSON, POUGHKEEPSIE, and throughout the state,
without regard to color, creed or sect, are earnestly solicited to come and participate with us on the
day we celebrate.

OH! FOR FREEDOM! Frederick Douglass, Esq., will be present and
attend the Convention. This distinguished orator and champion of liberty, will lecture at 7 1-2
o'clock P. M., in the Baptist Church, Hamilton St., between Fulton and Grand Sts. Subject: THE
PRESIDENT AND EMANCIPATION. A Festival Extraordinary will be prepared by the Ladies.

ADMISSION FIFTEEN CENTS TO DEFRAY EXPENSES.

The committee recommend the observance of the 5th day of January, as a holiday, and that all
business be suspended during the siting of the Convention, in honor of the proclamation of freedom.
Tickets for sale at the Bookstores and by the undersigned Committee of Arrangements.

STEPHEN MYERS,	J. A. SMITH,	F. VAN EPPS,
P. ROBINSON,	W. H. DIETZ,	J. R. JONES,
JACOB MASON,	R. WRITE,	J. P. JOHNSON,
M. W. PRICE,	WM. H. ANTHONY,	B. CUTLER,

WM. H. JOHNSON, Secretary, No. 27 Maiden Lane.

Today, Washington County photographer Clifford Oliver creates contemporary images of slavery to remind modern viewers of the scarcity of African Americans in photographs during the medium's earliest years. "As a photographer well informed about the history of photography and slavery," Oliver remarks, "I wanted to make photographs that put blacks back in history."

FROM BANK TO BANK: CROSSING THE HUDSON RIVER

Summer Crossings

While the Hudson River has provided excellent north-south travel opportunities, crossing the waterway laterally by boat, sleigh, bridge, or tunnel has been critical for the settlement and commercial development of the Hudson Valley. Prior to the construction of

THE FUGITIVE'S STORY
John Rogers (1829–1904)
Painted plaster, 1865
Gift of Mrs. Ledyard Cogswell Jr., Benjamin Arnold Collection, 1945.94.13
Photography by Gary Gold

bridges, residents and travelers relied on rafts, boats, and ferries that linked the east and west banks during the warmer months of the year. One of the earliest documented ferry services in the country operated between Albany and East Greenbush in 1642. Poled by hand and often aided by guide ropes, scows, as well as larger flat-bottomed boats or bateaus, were used to transport teams of horses and wagons. Horse-powered ferryboats became popular by the 1830s, followed by steam ferries about ten years later. More than thirty scheduled ferries operated on the river between New York City and Troy by 1900.

Winter Crossings

Ice formed regularly on the upper portions of the Hudson River until the 1930s, when deep channels were dredged for the year-round operation of the Port of Albany. A frozen river provided many opportunities to cross from one side to another. Numerous references to people walking or skating across survive, but horse-drawn sleighs provided one of the fastest and most common crossing methods. The popular Albany Sleigh, manufactured by James Goold and Company, was well known throughout the United States and Europe. According to an 1871–72 brochure, Goold used only the finest wood and steel in his Albany Sleigh, which featured pleasing combinations of colorful paint decorations and included the finest plush upholstery and carpets for interiors. Established in 1813, Goold's company also manufactured carriages, coaches, and wagons.

HAYING ON THE HUDSON SHOWING A ROPE FERRY
Will H. Low (1853–1932)
Watercolor on paper, 1870
Gift of Miss Mary B. Danaher, niece of the artist,
1968.47.98

SNOW SCENE IN ALBANY, NEW YORK.

Snow Scene in Albany, New York

Unidentified artist
Colored wood engraving on paper, 1850
u2005.19

Bridges and Tunnels

The engineering marvels of bridges and tunnels have regularly provided stunning visual sights in the Hudson Valley. The earliest bridge to span the Hudson River, a wooden railroad bridge built by the Saratoga and Rensselaer Railroad, opened at Troy in 1832. Albany received its first bridge, also a railroad bridge, more than thirty years later in 1866. Farther south on the Hudson River, the Alfred H. Smith Memorial Bridge (also known as the Castleton Cut-Off), a double-arched steel-and-concrete railroad bridge at Castleton-on-Hudson and Selkirk, opened in 1928.

Increased automobile traffic led to further construction of bridges and tunnels throughout the twentieth century. The earliest automobile crossing was the Bear Mountain Bridge, built with

CASTLETON CUT-OFF

ALFRED H. SMITH MEMORIAL BRIDGE

CASTLETON CUT-OFF ALFRED H. SMITH
MEMORIAL BRIDGE POSTER

Unidentified artist
Photomechanical print on paper, ca. 1923
Gift of the New York Central Railroad,
1959.130.179
Photography by Gary Gold

57

private money from the Harriman family; it was the largest suspension bridge in the world when it opened in 1924. Within three years, the Holland Tunnel (1927) connecting New York City and New Jersey opened, followed by the Lincoln Tunnel ten years later. Other notable bridges on the Hudson River include the Franklin D. Roosevelt Mid-Hudson Bridge (1930), the George Washington Bridge (1931), the Tappan Zee Bridge (1957), and the Collar City Bridge (1981). In 2009 a refurbished railroad bridge built in 1889 at Poughkeepsie became the world's highest pedestrian bridge.

General Washington's Hudson River Blockade

Not all Hudson River crossings facilitated travel; one impeded it. In 1778 a rare blockade of the river occurred during the American Revolution, when American forces stretched a massive iron chain between West Point and Constitution Island in an attempt to prevent British ships from sailing to Albany. General George Washington

GEORGE WASHINGTON
Ezra Ames (1768-1836)
Oil on canvas, 1826
Gift of the Gallery of Fine Arts, 1900.5.2

(*facing page*) IRON LINK FROM THE GREAT CHAIN
Sterling Iron Works, Orange County, NY
Wrought iron, 1778
Gift of Charles R. Webster
1831.1
Photography by Gary Gold

and the British general William Howe recognized the immense value of controlling the Hudson. With this in mind, Washington charged the Polish engineer Colonel Thaddeus Kosciusko with designing and building the citadel at West Point. In 1778 Washington also ordered Kosciusko to construct an iron chain to block passage of British warships.

The massive chain, made of 1,200 links of wrought iron, stretched 1,700 feet in length, weighed 65 tons, and took 40 men a total of four days to install. Though the chain was never tested by British warships, West Point cadets have recently created a computer model and determined that in actuality it would not have stopped a ship at full sail.

Over the years, reproductions of the chain links were made and sold. In 1824 Charles R. Webster, publisher of the *Albany Gazette*, donated one of the original 1778 links to the Albany Institute. A ring of thirteen original links, representing the thirteen American colonies, attracts tourists on the grounds of West Point Military Academy.

STEREO VIEW OF THE CIRCLE OF 13 ORIGINAL IRON CHAINS AT TROPHY POINT, WEST POINT MILITARY ACADEMY

Published by Underwood & Underwood, Publishers, New York, London, Canada
Reproduction of photographic stereograph, 1901
Gift of W. Douglas McCombs

Sa Ga Yeath Qua Pieth Tow King of the Maquas

IMPORTING THE WORLD

New World Encounters Old

The 1609 arrival of the Dutch in the Hudson Valley initiated a long and complex relationship between Native Americans and Europeans (eventually Americans). Well before Europeans set foot on the continent, the native inhabitants of the Hudson Valley had established trade for materials collected from outside the region. During the years of European colonization, a network of trade and military allegiances aligned specific tribes with specific European colonizers. The Huron and French became allies, as did the Iroquois and British. Trade connections cemented friendships and established enemies.

Foodstuffs, tobacco, and land were some of the earliest commodities of exchange between Europeans and Native Americans, but the fashion for furs in Europe and the great abundance of beaver and other fur-bearing mammals in North America provided

SA GA YEATH QUA PIETH TOW, KING OF THE MAQUAS

Painted by Jan Verelst (fl. 1698–1734)
Engraved by John Simon
Mezzotint on paper, 1710
Gift of Mrs. Henry M. Sage, 1972.65.9
Photography by Joseph Levy

MOHAWK BEADED BAG SHOWN AT ALBANY RELIEF BAZAAR

Glass beads, wool and cotton cloth, 1864
Gift of Hildreth Houston Spencer in memory of her mother Cornelia
Hull Miller Spencer and her great-great aunt Elizabeth Frances Hull
1997.44.66
Photography by Gary Gold

Native Americans with their most sought-after trade product. In exchange for furs, natives received European goods such as cloth, metal pots, and knives.

Traditional Native American wampum beads made from clamshells served as a medium of exchange and symbol of friendship throughout the seventeenth century. When Peter Schuyler took four Indian chiefs to England in 1710 to reinforce political alliances with the British government, the Mohawk and Mahican Indians presented Queen Anne with wampum. By the middle of the 1700s, silver in the form of medals, armbands, and brooches became an important commodity traded to Native Americans or given by government officials as symbols or covenants of peace.

Following the American Revolution, the new government settled many Native Americans in the Northeast on land reserves or forced them west into unsettled territory, yet cultural and commercial interactions continued. Throughout the nineteenth century, northeastern natives frequently sold baskets town to town, and beaded bags and birch bark souvenirs at fairs and resorts like Saratoga Springs. The production of Native American crafts keeps cultural exchange alive in the twenty-first century while preserving age-old traditions and customs.

Goods from Around the World

For four hundred years, the Hudson River has connected the people of its valley to the world beyond America's shores. Imported beverages, containers, and serving utensils from the Netherlands, central Europe, England, India, China, and the Caribbean filled shops and homes throughout the region. At the site of Fort Orange in Albany's South End, archeological excavations have unearthed abundant shards of European ceramics, revealing that seventeenth-century Dutch soldiers and traders drank from Dutch earthenware cups and poured their beer from German stoneware jugs, even in the wilds of the New World.

By the end of the seventeenth century, Chinese porcelains entered the households of prominent Hudson Valley families. The 1695 will of Albany resident Margaret Van Varick lists "1 China cupp bound with silver." The silver mounts on the cup highlight the preciousness of Chinese porcelains at this early date. Families owned complete tea and dinner sets from China by 1800, some arriving on the small Albany sloop *Experiment*, which set sail for Asia in 1785 and returned eighteen months later loaded with porcelain, tea, and silk cloth.

The Industrial Revolution in England transformed British potteries into manufacturing powerhouses by the last quarter of the eighteenth century. In Staffordshire and other counties in England

Tea box from WGY Food Products Co. of Schenectady
Photomechanical printed paper over wood, metal, and plastic,
ca. 1920–1940
2006.7
Photography by Gary Gold

64

French neoclassical clock purchased by
Stephen Van Rensselaer IV in France

Unidentified maker, France
Marble, brass, ormolu, enamel, and glass, ca. 1813
Gift of Mr. and Mrs. Arnold Cogswell, 1967.37
Photography by Gary Gold

and Scotland, potters produced such large quantities of dinner wares and tea services that British earthenware ceramics became eminently affordable and available as imports throughout the Hudson Valley.

Merchants today continue to stock shelves with imported beverages and ceramics, maintaining the Hudson Valley's enduring connection to the world.

Importing Style

Along with products and people, the Hudson River has moved ideas and information; it has allowed for the flow of styles and design trends from Europe and Asia. An interest in ancient Greek and Roman art, architecture, and culture in the late eighteenth and early nineteenth centuries, fueled by excavations at the Italian sites of Pompeii and Herculaneum, filtered into America with tourists, artists, merchants, and immigrants, who brought to the Hudson Valley neoclassical home furnishings, artwork, and fashions. In 1813 Stephen Van Rensselaer IV of Albany traveled through France and returned home with an ornate clock decorated with neoclassical design elements, topped by a gilded statue of the Roman goddess Minerva. Four years later, he and his new bride, Harriet Bayard, received neoclassical furniture made by the French immigrant cabinetmaker Charles-Honoré Lannuier of New York City.

PORTRAIT OF MARIA VAN SCHAICK
Ezra Ames (1768–1836), Albany
Oil on canvas, ca. 1808
Gift of the Estate of Mary Louise Peebles, 1915.1.5
Photography by Gary Gold

Nearly all women in the early 1800s favored white cotton dresses like that worn by Maria Van Schaick of Albany in her portrait painted by Ezra Ames. The style, which imitated the ancient Greek chiton as seen on Greek vases and bas-relief sculptures, was one of the most prominent expressions of the neoclassical style.

The 1853 opening of Japan as a trading center by American naval officer Matthew Perry introduced Japanese arts and culture to the Western world, creating a fad for Japanese goods and design. Albany lawyer Robert Hewson Pruyn, appointed second minister to Japan in 1861 by Abraham Lincoln, sent home prints and photographs of Japanese buildings that disseminated Japanese aesthetics at an early date. By the 1870s and 1880s, Japanese parasols, fans, screens, and ceramics commonly appeared in American homes such as Appledale, the summer residence of Albany sculptor Erastus Dow Palmer.

JAPANESE FAN

Unidentified artist
Silk and wood, ca. 1919
x1940.27.27
Photography by Gary Gold

DINING ROOM AT APPLEDALE

Walter Launt Palmer (1854–1932), Albany
Oil on canvas in original gilt frame, 1877
Gift of the heirs of the estate of
Robert W. Olcott
1947.56.3
Photography by Gary Gold

NOVEMBER 15, 1932

Wharves and Port

Commercial activity has characterized the Hudson River waterfront since the early seventeenth century. Wharves, docks, and ports have facilitated the transshipment of goods and people from river to land and vice versa; they have also been points of warehousing and manufacturing.

In 1794 the proprietors of Albany's wharves formed a joint-stock company to provide upkeep and collect duties legislated by the city. According to the company's minutes, the wharves originally extended from the middle of Maiden Lane to the north side of State Street. Keeping track of the duties collected, projects undertaken, and dividends paid to stockholders required care. In 1811 the

GLEN S. COOK
ALBANY, N.Y.

ALBANY

PANORAMIC PHOTOGRAPH OF THE PORT OF ALBANY

Glen S. Cook
Silver gelatin photographic print, 1932
Manuscript collection, MG 16

proprietors presented John Van Schaick, the company's clerk, with a silver tray for his attentive recordkeeping, underlining the importance of managing city's waterfront.

President Calvin Coolidge transformed Albany's waterfront when he signed legislation in 1924 to dredge the Hudson River for ocean-going ships. Later that year he created the Albany Port District Commission. Construction of Albany's port began two years later. On June 7, 1932, Governor Franklin Delano Roosevelt dedicated the completed $18 million project, which included warehouses, grain storage, rail connections, wharves, and a deepwater shipping channel. The Port of Albany continues to serve the regional economy by handling goods such as windmill blades, pipe, grain, and molasses.

69

HUDSON RIVER LANDING
Albertus del Orient Browere (1814–1887), Oil on wood panel in gilt frame, ca. 1840
Gift of J. Townsend Lansing
X1940.590.80
Photography by Joseph Levy

HARMONY COMPANY MILLS,
COHOES, NEW YORK

John J. New
Albumen photographic print on card, ca. 1870
Stereo view collection

John H. New, Photographer,

31 Remsen Street, Cohoes, N. Y.

EXPORTING THE VALLEY

Textiles

The Hudson Valley has been a manufacturing powerhouse for hundreds of years, producing industrial products and consumer goods for use locally and around the world. Several factors have contributed to its prominence, including a wealth of natural resources, significant sources of power, critical transportation connections, and an enterprising and persevering labor force. All of these coalesced at the juncture of the Mohawk and Hudson Rivers in the early nineteenth century. Cohoes Falls supplied waterpower to operate factories and mills, and the Erie Canal and Hudson River offered easy transportation.

In 1825 Stephen Van Rensselaer III and Canvass White founded the Cohoes Company, which bought the rights to waterpower generated from the falls. Within ten years, the company was selling both waterpower and mill privileges. Water eventually powered dozens of textile mills and machine shops in Cohoes. One of these mills, the Harmony Company, founded in 1837, became the largest cotton-

textile mill in the world. In 1872 it used 250,000 pounds of cotton per week to produce 1,256,000 yards of cloth and employed nearly 4,000 workers, more than 2,500 of whom were women. Immigrants from Ireland and French Canada figured prominently in labor force; many lived in tenement houses constructed near the mills.

In Troy, across the river from Cohoes, Ebenezer Brown opened a small factory to make detachable collars in 1829. The industry eventually grew to such prominence that Troy was nicknamed the "Collar City." In 1893 the *North American Review* remarked, "All the really well dressed people you meet wear Troy collars, cuffs, and shirts." Factories in the city made seventeen million collars in 1910. As detachable collars declined in fashion, Cluett, Peabody, and Company transitioned to shirts and remained in Troy until 1990.

Iron

Throughout the nineteenth century, iron foundries operated in the Hudson Valley from New York City to Lake Sanford in the Adirondacks and produced great quantities of iron goods. Nearly all the raw materials, including iron ore, limestone for flux, forests for charcoal (later replaced with coal via the Delaware and Hudson Canal), casting sand, and waterpower to pump furnace bellows, came from local sources.

In 1818 the West Point Foundry Association began casting armaments at Cold Spring in the mid-Hudson Valley. It was one of four foundries subsidized by the U.S. government. At the time of the Civil War, the foundry employed 1,400 men and in addition to armaments cast garden benches, pipe, and equipment for West Indian sugar mills.

Farther north, Scottish immigrant Henry Burden established his own foundry in Troy. By 1835 Burden patented a machine to cast horseshoes, which he continually refined over the years until his foundry could cast one horseshoe per second. Also in Troy, the Rensselaer Iron Foundry produced the iron panels for the USS *Monitor*, the first ironclad ship used in the Civil War.

Albany and Troy also became world leaders in cast-iron stove manufacturing during the nineteenth century. By the 1850s, seven foundries, employing 1,700 workers and producing more than $2 million worth of stoves annually, prospered in these two cities. Within another twenty-five years, fifteen stove manufacturers operated in Albany and seventeen in Troy, with a combined annual value of stoves reaching a staggering $5.8 million. Stoves cost

TERRIFIC ENGAGEMENT BETWEEN THE "MONITOR" 2 GUNS, AND "MERRIMAC" 10 GUNS, IN HAMPTON ROADS, MARCH 9TH 1862.
The First Fight between Iron Ships of War,
In which the Merrimac was crippled, and the whole Rebel Fleet driven back to Norfolk.

TERRIFIC ENGAGEMENT BETWEEN THE
"MONITOR" 2 GUNS, AND "MERRIMAC" 10 GUNS,
IN HAMPTON ROADS, MARCH 9TH 1862

Printed by Nathaniel Currier (1813–1888) and
James Merritt Ives (1824–1895), New York City
Colored lithograph on paper, 1862
1961.68
Photography by Gary Gold

(facing page)
TWO-COLUMN PARLOR STOVE

Pratt & Treadwell, Albany
Cast iron, ca. 1834–1836
1967.29
Photography by Gary Gold

between $4 and $40 apiece in 1875, making them affordable for most homeowners. Albany foundry owners such as Joel Rathbone and the partnership of Elisha N. Pratt and John G. Treadwell of Albany produced stoves that were beautiful, useful, and in many cases technologically innovative.

The development of steel in the later nineteenth century led to the decline of Hudson Valley iron production. Only a few foundries remained in business into the next century; one of these, the Albany Foundry, specialized in small decorative items, primarily bookends and doorstops.

Building Materials

Glacial deposits of clay and lime from a vast prehistoric inland sea have made the Hudson River valley an important center for brick and cement making. Stone and marble quarries at Peekskill and Sing-Sing further supplied the building trades, supported by New York City and its great need for construction materials.

Hudson Valley brick making began in the seventeenth century with the Dutch, who brought to the region their preference for brick houses. Two hundred years later, brickyards flourished in the Hudson Valley. Because of its superb blue-clay deposits, Haverstraw was the center of brick production. In 1852 Haverstraw resident Richard Ver Valen developed a packing machine that firmly pressed clay into molds. His invention facilitated brick making, such that forty-one manufacturers operated in Haverstraw by the end of the century, producing 325 million bricks per year. Brick factories stretched

NEWARK LIME & CEMENT
MANUFACTURING CO.'S WORKS,
RONDOUT, NEW YORK
Unidentified printer
Colored lithograph on paper, 1880
u1977.146
Photography by Gary Gold

NEWARK LIME & CEMENT MANUFACTURING CO'S WORKS. RONDOUT, NEW YORK. JAMES G. LINDSLEY, AGT.

north from Haverstraw to Saugerties, Coeymans, Castleton, and Mechanicville. In Albany, brickyards such as James C. Moore's made bricks for building construction and road paving.

In addition to brickworks, kilns to burn lime for the production of mortar and cement lined the Hudson River during the nineteenth century. The Newark Lime and Cement Manufacturing Company was one of several that thrived around Kingston. It initially quarried limestone from a Rondout, New York, mine for its factory in Newark, New Jersey, but from 1851 to 1929 it also manufactured cement in Rondout.

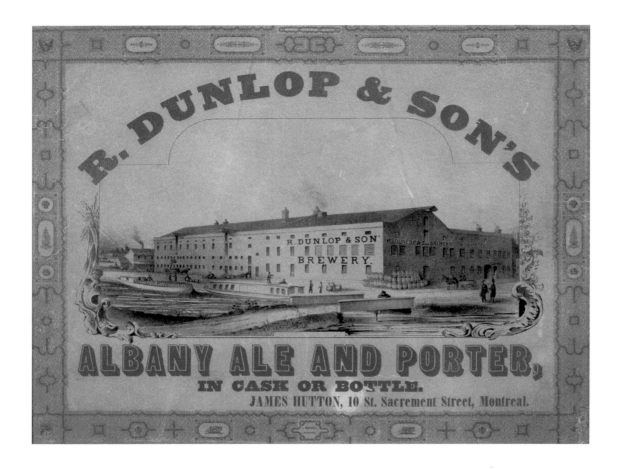

R. DUNLOP & SON'S ALBANY ALE AND
PORTER, IN CASK OR BOTTLE.

Printed by Joel Munsell, Albany
Lithograph and letterpress on paper, ca. 1840
Bequest of Ledyard Cogswell Jr.
1954.59.10
Photography by Gary Gold

Brewing

In 1632 the Dutch patroon Kiliaen Van Rensselaer wrote, "As soon as there is a supply of grain on hand, I intend to erect a brewery to provide all New Netherland with beer." Brewing began the following year and continued on a small scale until the 1800s. It was one of the earliest industries in the Hudson Valley.

When Thomas McKenney, the U.S. superintendent of Indian affairs, passed through Albany in 1826, he noticed the prominence of breweries, which produced nearly $200,000 worth of beer annually. English immigrant John Taylor established a brewery in Albany that became the largest in the United States; a local newspaper reported in 1825 that the Taylor brewery produced 250 barrels of beer daily. Even accusations from prohibitionist Edward C. Delavan, owner of Delavan's hotel, that Taylor used contaminated water did not stop the growth of his business. Taylor's brewery operated until 1910.

BEVERWYCK BREWING COMPANY SERVING TRAY

Printed and painted sheet iron, ca. 1900
Gift of Ivan C. and Marilynn Karp
2005.18.6
Photography by Gary Gold

HEDRICK'S BEER SIX-PACK

Photomechanical printed cardboard
and aluminum, ca. 1960
Gift of Anna Cipollo
1994.23.1
Photography by Joseph Levy

Other brewing facilities opened in the region, including the Quinn and Nolan Brewery, established in 1866. Quinn and Nolan initially brewed English-style ales and porters but in 1878 opened Beverwyck Brewery, a subsidiary that specialized in German-style lager, in response to the increasing numbers of German immigrants in the United States. Beverwyck and Hedrick breweries survived Prohibition in the 1920s, but the F. and M. Schaefer Brewing Company of New York bought Beverwyck in 1950, and Hedrick's closed in 1965.

In the late twentieth century, the opening of locally owned microbreweries initiated a brewing revival. Today microbreweries handcraft high-quality brews in limited quantities.

Nanotechnology

Working at the scale of one-billionth of a meter, nanoscale science and technology manage and manipulate matter at the atomic level in order to create products and systems that better the world.

The College of Nanoscale Science and Engineering (CNSE) of the University at Albany–State University of New York is recognized as a global leader in this technological revolution. CNSE represents a

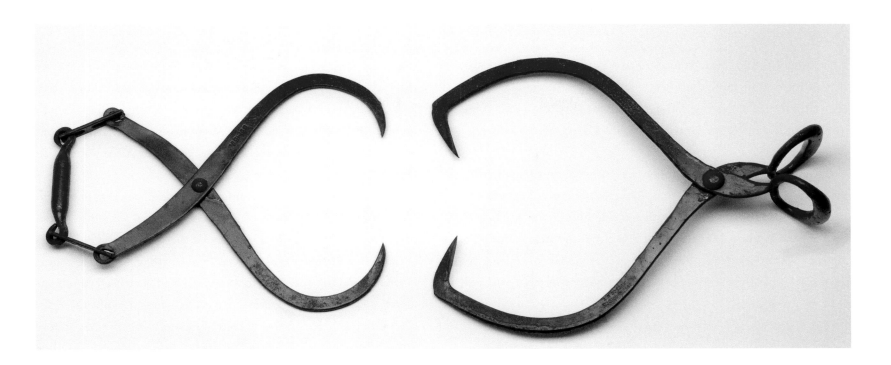

ICE TONGS FOR HAULING ICE BLOCKS UP AN INCLINED PLANE
AND LOADING AND UNLOADING VESSELS
Manufactured by Gifford Ice Company, Hudson, NY
Painted metal, ca. 1900
Gift of Derek Plass
2003.50.3 and 2003.50.4
Photography by Gary Gold

combined vision of government, academia, and industry, with a common goal to propel New York State to a leadership position in nanotechnology education, research, and economic development.

Products ranging from sophisticated computer chips that speed the flow and processing of information to vital alternative energy technologies exist because of nanotechnology. Nanoscale science also allows manufacturers to build better and more durable products, such as L. L. Bean's stain-repellent "Double L Chinos," and enhances leisure time and sports activities by making possible interactive video games, digital music players, and more-responsive golf balls.

RIVER AS PRODUCT: ICE HARVESTING

Ice Harvesting on the Hudson River
Harvesting ice from the Hudson River and nearby ponds, lakes, and canals flourished as a major industry from 1860 to about 1910. The ice was sold locally, in New York City, and as far away as India

and China. In 1880, 135 icehouses dotted the banks of the Hudson River; thirty years later there were almost 200. At the height of the natural-ice harvesting industry, over twenty thousand men worked seasonally from January to early March, along with one thousand horses.

While some ice-harvesting operations were quite small, others built mammoth icehouses that used elevators or pulley systems to transport the blocks or cakes of ice inside for storage. Ice barges traveled the Hudson River during the warmer months, transporting ice to a variety of facilities for local and global shipments. In later years, many of the wooden icehouses burned or were used for growing mushrooms.

Depending on the weather conditions, labor force, and equipment, it took between ten and twenty days to fill a large icehouse. Specialized tools and machinery aided the harvest. Snowplows or scrapers removed the snow; ice markers, cutters, and saws cut the ice; and ice hooks, chisels, and hoisting tongs moved it. Special steel spikes called ice creepers helped the workers and horses to walk on the slippery surface.

A horse-pulled "shine sled" driven by a "shine boy" was responsible for picking up the horse droppings, referred to as "diamonds." A quick scraping of the ice followed by a dose of formaldehyde helped to purify it. Once in the icehouse, sawdust-covered ice could last up to three years.

Natural Ice versus Artificial Ice

By the early twentieth century, an advanced understanding of disease pathology coupled with growing concerns about pollution and poor sanitation systems placed natural ice at the center of public alarm about contagious diseases, especially cholera, typhoid, and tuberculosis. High levels of bacteria from sewage and other industrial pollutants caused the New York State commissioner of health to condemn ice harvested from the Hudson River near Albany and other locations.

As the anxiety over contaminated natural ice grew, new companies devised a process to manufacture artificial ice, raising a debate. Proponents of natural ice claimed their product lasted longer because it was formed over time, and they further asserted that prolonged periods of freezing temperatures killed bacteria. Proponents of artificial ice, on the other hand, stated that manufactured ice was more hygienic and free of contaminants. Advertisements from artificial-ice companies often included pictures of horses standing on the ice with "diamonds," or manure, nearby to persuade customers to buy their hygienic ice.

Refrigeration

The use of ice or snow for food preservation and cooling dates back to ancient Greece and Rome. In America during the colonial era, icehouses insulated with salted hay and filled with large blocks of ice were common in both rural and urban areas. During this time people used ice sparingly, mainly to cool dairy products and beverages, but affluent families also used ice to chill wine glasses, often in specially designed bowls called monteiths. Made of silver or ceramic, a monteith had a distinctive indented rim that supported the stems of wine glasses while suspending the bowls in ice or chilled water.

Advertisement for Hygienic Ice & Refrigerating Co.

From *Albany City Directory*
Letterpress on paper, 1910
Library collection

Advertisement for Hudson Valley Ice Co.

From *Albany City Directory*
Letterpress on paper, 1910
Library collection

MONTEITH BOWL

Unidentified maker, England
Tin-glazed earthenware, ca. 1725
Gift of Herbert L. Shultz and
Eleanor Shultz Adams
1995.22.1
Photography by Gary Gold

In 1793 a Maryland farmer obtained a patent for an icebox he used to transport butter to his customers. Since that time, a variety of large and small icebox and refrigerator designs were developed. Most, made of wood, had insulated walls filled with charcoal, cork, flax, or wool and interior linings of zinc, slate, porcelain, or galvanized metal.

As faster transportation systems and more reliable refrigeration techniques developed, the demand for natural ice increased in order to service the growing markets for fresh produce, meat, and dairy products. In cities and towns, icemen delivered their frozen product by horse and wagon. A block of ice would usually last a day or two in these early iceboxes; water from the melting ice drained into a pan to be emptied or was piped outside. By 1915 electric- and gas-powered refrigerators manufactured by Frigidaire, General Electric, and other firms made their debut. Refrigeration significantly changed the food industry in terms of the type and quantity of fresh food available, and it enabled industries such as brewing and meatpacking to operate year round.

FISH TALES

Fish in Abundance

The number and variety of fish found in the Hudson River is astounding—scientists have identified 210 species. As a tidal estuary, the Hudson, with its mix of saltwater and freshwater, is among the most productive ecosystems on the planet. Salt tides reach as far north as Poughkeepsie, and both marine and freshwater species live in the river.

On September 15, 1609, Robert Juet, Henry Hudson's first mate on board the ship *Half Moon*, recorded in his journal that "the river was full of fish." Twelve days later, Juet wrote that after fishing for an hour, twenty-four or twenty-five fish were caught, including "mullets, breams, basses and barbils." Among other early eyewitness accounts, Adriaen van der Donck sighted several whales in the river in 1647 near the present-day city of Troy. Porpoises and dolphins were also commonly seen south of Albany until the nineteenth century. Notable "marine strays" in the Hudson River include sharks, skates, conger eels, and Atlantic cod. Common year-round or seasonal fish include bass, perch, bluefish, shad, sturgeon, herring, carp, needlefish, golden shiners, darters, tomcod, and sunfish.

Albany Beef, or A Sturgeon's Story

The oceangoing Atlantic sturgeon is the largest fish to inhabit the Hudson River. Of prehistoric origin, the sturgeon has distinctive bony, armored plates, can weigh up to eight hundred pounds, and occasionally measures fourteen feet in length. Sturgeons are bottom feeders that use sensitive, whisker-like barbels on the undersides of their snouts to find food, chiefly worms, insects, crustaceans, and small fish, which they suck into their tube-like mouths.

Large Atlantic sturgeons were once so plentiful in Hudson River markets that early-nineteenth-century residents of the Hudson Valley referred them as "Albany beef." The decorator of an 1809 stoneware butter churn made in Albany at the pottery of Paul Cushman knew well the sturgeon's regional identity; he depicted a cow suckling a sturgeon, making a visual joke on the name "Albany beef." Not only were sturgeon fished for food, but their caviar was also highly prized. In 1991 a seven-ounce jar of Hudson Caviar sold for $119; in 2000 one ounce sold for $100. Hyde Park, New York, a known spawning ground for sturgeon, developed as an important processing center for sturgeon flesh and roe. Today the area is monitored by scientists who assess the species' viability.

In an effort to protect sturgeon for future generations, Atlantic coast states from Maine to Florida declared a forty-year fishing moratorium in 1998. Nowadays the distinctive image of the Atlantic sturgeon appears as the logo for New York State Department of Environmental Conservation's Hudson River Estuary Program.

Commercial Fishing

For years, people living along the Hudson have fished the river and its tributaries for food. American shad fishing is one of the oldest traditional industries found in the Hudson Valley. Each spring American shad (*Alosa sapidissima*, meaning "shad most delicious") leave the Atlantic Ocean to spawn in the Hudson River. The season begins when the lilacs and shadblow trees bloom.

In order to help preserve the species, plans to impose stricter regulations on commercial shad fishing in the Hudson are currently underway. Over the years, the effects of dams, channel dredging, pollutants, and the increased efficiency of fishing have severely reduced the numbers of all fish in the river.

BUTTER CHURN WITH COW SUCKLING A STURGEON

Paul Cushman (1767–1833), Albany
Salt-glazed stoneware with cobalt decoration, 1809
Gift of John P. Remensnyder
1977.20.4
Photography by Michael Fredericks

(*facing page*) BROOK TROUT FISHING

Painted by Arthur F. Tait (1819–1905)
Drawn by Charles Parsons (1821–1910)
Printed by Nathaniel Currier (1813–1888) and James Merritt
Ives (1824–1895), New York City
Colored lithograph on paper, 1862
Bequest of Milton Alexander
1975.12.2
Photography by Gary Gold

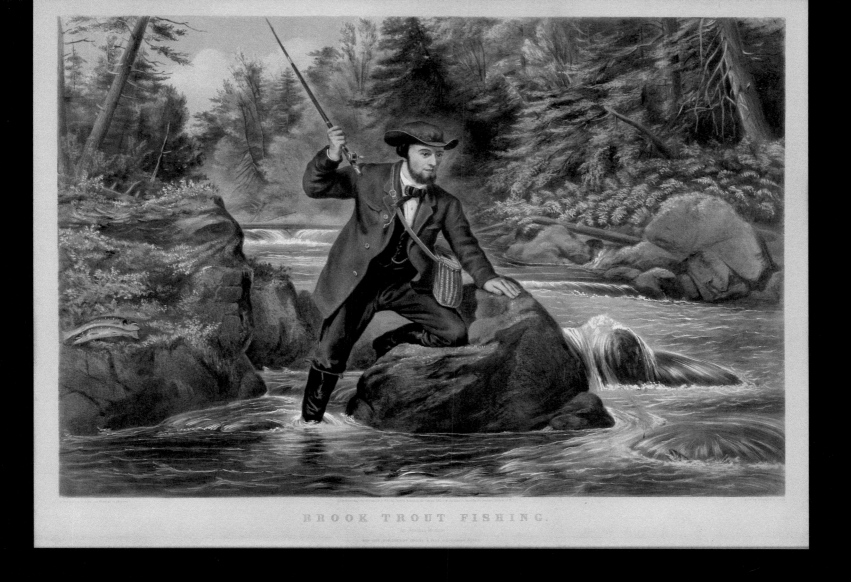

BROOK TROUT FISHING.

Sport Fishing

The Hudson River and its tributaries provide ample opportunities for the recreation and competition of sport fishing. The well-known late-nineteenth-century fly fisherman and sporting writer Theodore Gordon helped establish the Catskills as a prime fishing area in the Northeast, even designing and popularizing a selection of flies specifically for the region. Gordon and others led a campaign to designate the Catskills as the birthplace of American fly fishing. Gordon's flies, small artificial lures made from natural fur, feathers, and yarn tied onto tiny hooks to imitate insects and larvae, were some of the

earliest American-specific fly designs (rather than the copies of British flies that most Americans used at the time). In the twentieth century, longtime Albany mayor Erastus Corning II enjoyed fly fishing in the region, thanks in part to the work of Gordon.

Today the striped bass is one of the top game fish in the Hudson River. Like American shad, Atlantic striped bass swim up the river as far as Troy each spring, attracting anglers from around the world. These hard-fighting fish can weigh up to forty pounds. In 1976 a commercial ban on striped bass fishing was imposed because of high levels of PCBs, industrial chemicals linked to cancer, in the river. While the pollution levels have decreased significantly, new regulations adopted in 2008 further limit the commercial and sport harvest to help protect the fish as well as consumers. Other sport-fishing opportunities include the popular annual trout- and bass-fishing tournaments and derbies.

Whaling and the Romance of the Sea

In 1783 a group of Quaker whalers from Nantucket Island known as the "Nantucket Navigators" sailed up the Hudson River looking for a new whaling port. They were seeking to avoid paying the tariffs imposed by the British for whale oil following the American Revolution. The community of Hudson, located on the east bank of the river opposite the Catskill Mountains, became the base of their

SHAD-FISHING ON THE HUDSON

From the *Illustrated London News*, August 7, 1875
Wood engraving on paper
u1990.163

whaling activities. This initial venture proved short lived, but whaling returned to Hudson again in 1830 for another fifteen years. As the demand for whale oil for use in lamps, as candle wax, and as lubrication for machinery increased, so too did the demand for baleen, a flexible material found in the mouths of right whales that was used to make corsets stays, hoopskirts, umbrella and parasol ribbing, and riding whips. The city of Hudson became the most successful whaling port on the Hudson River, but whaling companies also thrived in Poughkeepsie and Newburgh.

The allure of adventure and the possibility of lucrative earnings prompted many young men to join whaling ships in the nineteenth century. In 1829 Alonzo Wheeler, a wagon maker from Chatham, New York, moved to Hudson and joined the whaler *Martha.* In his journal, Wheeler wrote that the crew "killed and saved our first and second whales," and, an another occasion, "took a whale." Wheeler's decision to go to sea was likely influenced by the popularity and proliferation of romantic stories about life on the ocean. Such was the case for young Isaac Newton Eddy of Waterford, New York, who ran away to sea on the whaling vessel *Hector.* He eventually contracted disease—a fate common to many

PARASOL WITH BALEEN RIBS
Unidentified maker
Silk, metal, and baleen, 1845–1850
Benjamin W. Arnold collection
1985.11
Photography by Gary Gold

87

ISAAC NEWTON EDDY MEMORIAL
ON COMORO ISLAND, INDIAN OCEAN

Ralph A. Savage (1827–1904), Waterford, NY
Oil on canvas, 1855
Gift of Albert B. Roberts
2006.49.5
Photography by Gary Gold

REST STOP

young crew members—and died near the Comoro Islands, off the coast of Madagascar. When he died, Eddy was aboard the ship *Eleanor* bound for home, and his body was taken ashore and buried. A fellow sailor on the ship, Walter A. Kizar, made a sketch of the spot where young Eddy was buried. When Eddy's family received the sketch, they commissioned Waterford artist Ralph Savage to create a memorial painting, which kept alive the memory of Isaac Newton Eddy while cautioning other young men of the perils of whaling.

The First Great Resort Hotel

For centuries, inns, hotels, and taverns have furnished room and board for travelers in the Hudson Valley. These places of rest and refreshment have contributed to the regional economy and identity. Some hotels such as the Catskill Mountain House, also known as Pine Orchard, attracted artists, writers, and tourists who admired spectacular scenery.

The construction of the Catskill Mountain House was a result of several developments and cultural processes underway by the 1820s,

CATSKILL MOUNTAIN HOUSE

DeWitt Clinton Boutelle (1820–1884)
Oil on canvas in gilt frame, 1845
1975.20
Photography by Gary Gold

namely regular and inexpensive steamboat travel, admiration of the American wilderness by artists and writers, and the rise of urban-based professionals and merchants who had the financial means to travel for pleasure. In 1823 a group of investors purchased three hundred acres of land on the eastern ridge of the Catskills and the following year opened the Mountain House, a small hotel two thousand feet above the valley below and forty feet from the mountain's edge. It looked

eastward onto an expansive scene, and throughout the nineteenth century the hotel attracted multitudes of tourists, who enjoyed the view from the piazza, the scenery of North and South Lakes just to the west, and the various waterfalls at Kaaterskill Clove.

Charles L. Beach, the owner of a stagecoach line running from Catskill Landing to the Mountain House, bought the hotel in 1845. Beach recognized the profits to be gained by co-owning

transportation lines and a resort hotel. In 1882 he built the Catskill Mountain Railroad, leading from the Hudson River to the base of the mountain, and ten years later his Otis Elevated Railroad took visitors directly up the mountain to his hotel.

Attendance at the Catskill Mountain House declined in the years after 1918. The hotel closed following the 1942 season, and the building suffered considerable structural damage during a hurricane that passed through the Catskills on November 26, 1950. It sat de- caying until the New York State Conservation Department deemed it a safety hazard and burned it to the ground on January 25, 1963.

Amenities for Travelers

The community of Albany grew and prospered at the crossroads of a far-reaching commercial and transportation network that began in the early 1600s. Over the centuries, traders, merchants, politicians, and tourists have traveled to the city or passed through en route to other destinations. In order to meet the needs of these transitory visitors, numerous hotels and inns have operated in the region.

Accessibility and comfort, the two main attractions of most hotels, became key elements in their marketing strategies. An advertisement for Albany's Mansion House hotel noted in 1873 that it was "one block and a-half from steamboat landing, and the direct route to all the railroad depots." The Mansion House, like other hotels, was strategically located close to the major arteries of transportation. Hotels also emphasized restaurants, ballrooms, reading rooms, lounges, and homelike comforts. The Cataract House, situated just below Cohoes Falls, took advantage of the scenery but also noted its proximity to the Shaker Village in Watervliet, a tourist destination, and the fact that its ballroom could accommodate sleighing parties.

In 1845 Edward C. Delavan, a temperance advocate and abolitionist, opened the Delavan House on Broadway in Albany; the hotel was patronized by New York's anti-liquor legislators and was also the unofficial headquarters for both the Democratic and Republican political parties. Abraham Lincoln lodged at Delavan's in 1861 on his way to Washington, D.C., for his inauguration.

Hotels continue to serve the Capital Region today. Situated near highways, airports, and centers of business and politics instead of river landings and railroads, they provide accommodations for thousands of travelers each year.

(this page)
DeWitt Clinton Hotel trade card

Ink on paper, c. 1930
Trade card collection

(facing page)
Mansion House, Albany

Frederick Swinton
Lithograph on paper, 1845
Bequest of Ledyard Cogswell Jr.
1954.59.9
Photography by Gary Gold

DRAWN & ON STONE BY F.J.SWINTON   J.H.HALL LITH. ALBANY, N.Y.

MANSION HOUSE, ALBANY.

Nº 22 & 24 BROADWAY.   FRANKLIN LATHROP.

93

CATARACT HOUSE, COHOES FALLS, N. Y.

THE ATTRACTIONS.

Parties visiting this section of the Country should make it a special object to visit these "FALLS," it being one of the grandest sights for miles around. The CATARACT HOUSE is beautifully situated upon a bluff overlooking the Falls, and from its Observatory the Country can be seen for miles around. It is one of the most delightful places we know of, the cool breeze from the Falls always mitigating the intensity of the heat.

THE FALLS ARE THREE MILES FROM TROY, EIGHT FROM ALBANY, and but a short distance from SHAKER VILLAGE.

No expense has been spared to make the Cataract "Excelsior," in addition to the beautiful scenery surrounding the same. The artificial Fall 123 feet, the Falls of the "Mighty Mohawk" 86 feet, the Walk in the Dell, on the bed of the river, &c., &c., combine to make this a very attractive resort.

Pleasure Gondolas are on the Pond near the Cataract House; the Scenery from the many windows in the large Billiard Room is surprisingly beautiful, and a spacious Ball Room for the accommodation of Sleighing Parties is attached to the House.

Dinners and Suppers served in the most *recherche* style, and the Stabling Department is complete.

A ride or walk through the Town of Cohoes, famous by its unexcelled water power and princely factories, business streets and churches, thronged with well-to-do people, cannot fail to favorably impress a stranger—adding City charms to the Cataract House, situated on the summit of Mohawk Street,—a secluded spot in Nature's Garden.

WM. H. GWYNN, *Proprietor.*

CATARACT HOUSE,
COHOES FALLS, N.Y.

Printed by Charles Magnus,
New York City
Colored lithograph and
letterpress on paper in
maple veneered frame, ca. 1867
2007.43
Photography by Gary Gold

CULTURE AND SYMBOL

RIP VAN WINKLE RETURNS FROM THE MOUNTAINS

Tompkins Matteson (1813–1884)
Oil on canvas in gilt frame, 1860
1993.6
Photography by Gary Gold

RIP VAN WINKLE'S NEW YORK

Hudson Valley Tales

During the nineteenth century, American writers began to look back on the history of the Hudson Valley and its significance in shaping regional and national cultural identities. The Hudson River's central role in New York's Dutch colonial history, the Revolutionary War, and the growth of commerce and industry provided writers such as Washington Irving with captivating subjects and legendary, enduring characters who have come to be associated with the region.

Most people know the story of Rip Van Winkle, the lovable comic vagabond who wanders away from the drudgery of chores in his small Dutch village to the Catskill Mountains, only to return twenty years later with the excuse that he has just awakened after drinking from the flagon of Hendrick Hudson. When he returns, Rip Van Winkle finds his village utterly changed.

(*this page*)
WASHINGTON IRVING AND
HIS LITERARY FRIENDS AT
SUNNYSIDE

Christian Schessele (d. 1879)
Mezzotint on paper, 1864
1997.9.1
Photography by Gary Gold

(*facing page*)
RIP VAN WINKLE HOUSE,
CATSKILL MOUNTAINS

John Loeffler
Albumen photographic print
on card, ca. 1870
Stereo view collection

First published in 1819, "Rip Van Winkle" is more than just a story about local personalities and changes in society; Rip Van Winkle is a literary hero who presided over the birth of the American nation, imagination, and consciousness. The story of Rip still thrives in American literary and folk culture, where his presence is commemorated in anthologies, pictorial representations, and tourist sites throughout the Hudson Valley. Readers continue to experience pleasure in Rip's escapade. His failure to tend his garden is, after all, an amusing fantasy or cautionary tale in which readers examine, indirectly, both cultural customs and human nature.

Washington Irving and Kindred Spirits

A fiction writer, essayist, poet, travel-book writer, biographer, and columnist, Washington Irving, who often wrote under a pseudonym such as Jonathan Oldstyle, Geoffrey Crayon, or Diedrich Knickerbocker, has been called the father of the American short story. Irving's tales and characters, as well as his beloved Gothic Revival cottage, Sunnyside, continue to evoke and excite interest in the Hudson Valley and its people.

Irving encouraged and inspired many American writers, including Nathaniel Hawthorne, Herman Melville, Henry Wadsworth Longfellow, and Edgar Allan Poe. Several European writers such as Sir Walter Scott, Lord Byron, and Charles Dickens also admired him. As America's first internationally recognized best-selling author, Irving advocated for literary writing to be considered a legitimate profession and argued for stronger laws to protect American writers from copyright infringement.

In 1839 Irving joined the staff of *The Knickerbocker, or New-York Monthly Magazine*, a literary journal founded in 1833 and published until 1865 under various titles. Contributors to the magazine are often referred to as the "Knickerbocker Writers."

Sleepless in the Catskills

An ever-present folk figure in the Hudson Valley, Rip Van Winkle is widely represented not only as Washington Irving's well-known literary figure but also as the unofficial cultural ambassador for the region. Both the character of Rip and Irving's pseudonym "Knickerbocker" have come to represent the Dutch heritage of New York's Hudson Valley. Today, schools, campgrounds, and bridges are named for Rip Van Winkle. The contemporary writer Joyce Carol Oates writes of Irving's characters in her essay "Rip Van Winkle": "So deeply imprinted have they become in the popular imagination, they strike us as mytho-poetic figures—timeless, archetypal, transcending the circumstances of their own creation."

RIVER OF NOSTALGIA

Remembering the American Revolution

Societies often look to the past to commemorate historical milestones, learn from earlier people, events, and ideas, and ease anxieties about present situations by engaging in nostalgic reveries of

idyllic times gone by. Several events and celebrations along the Hudson River have focused on the past for these reasons.

As both a dividing line and link between colonies, the Hudson held a strategic position throughout the American Revolution. Soon after signing a peace treaty in 1784, Americans and British alike began recording and commemorating the heroic deeds and confrontations of the war such as the Battle of Saratoga, which led to the defeat of British general John Burgoyne on the upper Hudson River in September 1777. Artists and writers memorialized the bravery of American troops as well as the selfless acts of certain civilians, including Lady Harriet Ackland, whose husband, British officer Major

John Dyke Ackland, was wounded and captured by American forces. In order to attend her husband, who was held at the American camp, Lady Harriet crossed the Hudson River and placed herself in enemy hands. The American officer, Major General Horatio Gates, acknowledged her bravery and united her with her husband.

Engraved for BARNARD's New Complete & Authentic HISTORY of ENGLAND.

Hamilton delin.

Goldar sculp.

The Unfortunate DEATH of MAJOR ANDRE

(Adjutant General to the English Army) at Head Quarters in New York, Octr. 2. 1780, who was found within the American Lines in the character of a Spy.

Other sites along the river received similar recognition, including the site near Tarrytown where a small group of American farmers captured British officer Major John André in the early autumn of 1780 after he received confidential maps and plans of American fortifications at West Point from traitor Benedict Arnold. Though General George Washington ordered André to be hanged as a spy, Americans valued his honesty and valor, whereas they remembered Arnold as a turncoat.

A few years after André's hanging, while diplomats negotiated peace in 1782 and 1783, Washington maintained headquarters on the Hudson River at Newburgh, in the Hasbrouck House. In 1850 it became the first historic-house museum open to the public as a tourist attraction. New York State and the federal government maintain other Revolutionary War sites in the Hudson Valley, which keep alive the history of America's military quest for independence.

THE UNFORTUNATE DEATH OF MAJOR ANDRE

Drawn by William Hamilton
Engraved by John Goldar
From Edward Barnard, *The New, Comprehensive and Complete History of England: From the Earliest Period of Authentic Information, to the Middle of the Year, MDCCLXXXIII* (London, England)
Mixed method print, 1783
2008.7
Photography by Gary Gold

THE HALF MOON

HENDRIK HUDSON

·HUDSON·FULTON·
CELEBRATION·1909

The 1909 Hudson-Fulton Celebration

Planned as a commemoration of Henry Hudson's arrival in the New World in 1609 and Robert Fulton's 1807 maiden voyage of his steamship *Clermont* (originally called the *North River*), the 1909 Hudson-Fulton Celebration was organized to praise America's past and promote its technological and industrial future. The celebration, which took four years of planning and cost more than one million dollars, culminated in spectacular festivities that included flotillas, historical pageants, electrical light shows, and exhibitions of American antiques at the Metropolitan Museum of Art and the Albany Institute and Historical and Art Society (now the Albany Institute of History & Art).

Several events of the celebration reflected upon the past. At the opening festivities on September 25, a replica of Henry Hudson's ship *Half Moon*, a gift from the Dutch government, sailed into New York Harbor accompanied by a replica of Robert Fulton's *Clermont*,

(this page)
HUDSON-FULTON CELEBRATION POSTCARD

Valentine & Sons Publishing Co., New York City
Trichromatic halftone engraving on paper, 1909
Postcard collection

(facing page)
WASHINGTON'S HEADQUARTERS

Unidentified artist
Oil on canvas, ca. 1886–1901
Gift of Ledyard Cogswell Jr., 1949.1.8
Photography by Gary Gold

made by the Staten Island Shipbuilding Company. Over the following week and a half, the two ships sailed north on the Hudson River, stopping at communities along the way.

On September 28 a parade in New York City, consisting of fifty-four floats that chronicled New York's history, joined marchers from various ethnic societies. Planners designed the parade to educate foreign-born immigrants about American history while simultaneously celebrating the nation's cultural diversity.

Other events of the celebration acknowledged new technologies. Wilbur Wright made four flights over New York Harbor in his amazing airplane, and electrical lights illuminated ships and city streets. The New York City celebration even included a synchronized color light display along Riverside Drive, made possible by a device called the "Ryan Scintillator."

(this page)
MANUFACTURERS NATIONAL BANK, TROY,
DECORATED FOR THE HUDSON-FULTON CELEBRATION

Unidentified photographer
Silver gelatin photographic print, 1909
Postcard collection, 2007.71.2

(facing page)
PLATE FROM THE HUDSON-FULTON BANQUET,
ASTOR HOTEL, NEW YORK, SEPTEMBER 29, 1909

L. Strauss and Sons, New York City
Porcelain, 1909
Promised gift of Norman S. Rice
Photography by Gary Gold

SEEING THE SITES: HUDSON RIVER TOURISM

The Hudson River Picturesque Tour

The combination of grand scenery, notable historic sites, and accessible transportation contributed to a thriving tourist trade in the Hudson River valley by the first quarter of the nineteenth century. In 1807, when describing his passage down the Hudson River, English traveler John Lambert observed, "Nature and art have both contributed to render its shores at once sublime and beautiful." Inspired in part by the contemporary British craze for landscape tourism, Lambert vocalized what most nineteenth-century tourists eagerly sought: stunning scenery, pleasant farmlands and gardens, and sites of historical significance. Together these elements created a picturesque landscape, one literally "resembling a picture."

By the time Lambert made his journey, Europeans and Americans had begun to appreciate the unique beauty of the American landscape. The Hudson Valley became part of a circular itinerary that began in New York City. Tourists journeyed up the Hudson River to Albany and then to Niagara Falls, to Quebec, and eventually back to the river via Lake Champlain. Similar to the European grand tour, the Hudson Valley tour offered opportunities for cross-cultural encounters and aesthetic discovery.

Prints of Hudson River views in portfolios, in books, and on English ceramics stimulated regional tourism. The demand for images also encouraged the French salon artists Victor de Grailly and Hippolyte-Louis Garnier to paint American landscapes based on print sources, such as Jacques-Gérard Milbert's *Itinéraire Pittoresque du Fleuve Hudson* and William Bartlett's views in *American Scenery* (1840).

Savvy art dealers shipped hundreds of their paintings to America and sold them at auction to aspiring middle-class buyers.

Today, through conservation efforts, much of the picturesque scenery of the Hudson Valley admired by early tourists has been protected, ensuring that twenty-first-century visitors can continue to find sources of inspiration and discovery.

The Springs

"Life at the springs is a perpetual festival." When this statement appeared in *Frank Leslie's Illustrated Newspaper* in 1859, Saratoga Springs was the queen of American resorts. It had nearly fifty hotels and boarding houses and was fortuitously situated near a transportation network of steamships and railroads. The town boasted tree-lined streets and parks illuminated with gas lamps; it had theaters, fancy shops, and a circular railroad amusement ride. Most prominently, Saratoga had mineral springs.

When Philip Schuyler cut a path from his house on the Hudson River to High Rock Spring in 1783, he opened Saratoga Springs to visitors. Twenty years later, Connecticut native Gideon Putnam built the first tavern in town and began laying out streets and diverting springs to ornate fountains. As early as 1822, the water from Congress Springs was bottled and sold around the world. Drinking the mineral waters remained a favored activity at Saratoga Springs, but by the 1820s most visitors also sought entertainment. Annual horse races

(facing page)
ENTRANCE TO THE HIGHLANDS ON THE HUDSON

Hippolyte-Louis Garnier (1802–1855), France
Oil on canvas in gilt frame, ca. 1845
Gift of Albert B. Roberts, 2006.49.6
Photography by Gary Gold

(this page)
PLATE WITH VIEW OF THE "HIGHLANDS, NORTH RIVER"

Joseph Stubbs, England
Transfer-printed earthenware, ca. 1820
Bequest of Marjorie Doyle Rockwell, 1995.30.31
Photography by Gary Gold

(*this page*) Saratoga Springs (detail)

Drawn by Jacques-Gérard Milbert (1766–1840)
From *Itinéraire Pittoresque du Fleuve Hudson*
Published by A. Georges, Paris, France
Lithograph on paper, 1828
1944.22.18
Photography by Gary Gold

(*facing page*)
Start of the Great Republic ($50,000.—.) Saratoga, N.Y.

The American News Company, New York
Photomechanical print on paper, ca. 1905
Scrapbook collection, LIB 2009.194

Start of the Great Republic ($ 50,000.— ,)   Saratoga, N. Y.

began in 1863 and continue to the present, making the Saratoga track the oldest horseracing venue in the United States.

Unlike other resorts, Saratoga Springs survived the Great Depression and World War II. Construction of the Interstate 87 Adirondack Northway in the 1960s kept Saratoga within easy reach of tourists, and in 1966 the opening of the Saratoga Performing Arts Center (SPAC) established a venue for concerts and other live per-

formances. Six weeks of horseracing lasting through Labor Day make Saratoga a popular destination in the twenty-first century.

Armchair Tourist

The charms of the Hudson River valley—its scenery and historic sites—have attracted multitudes of tourists from the early 1800s to the present. For the "armchair tourist" unable or little inclined

HORSE-SHOE BEND VIEWED FROM SUMMIT.

PINE HILL.

ULSTER COUNTY = VIEWED FROM SUMMIT.

VIEWED FROM MT. HOPE ULSTER COUNTY.

HIGH POINT MT. 3300 F.T. HIGH.

FRIDAY MTS.

MT. CORNELL 3920 FEET.

WITTENBERG MT. 3824 FEET.

CROSS MT. 3400 FEET.

SAMUELS POINT 3000 FEET.

DELAWARE COUNTY- VIEWED FROM THE SUMMIT.

HORSE=SHOE BEND.

BELLE AYRE MOUNTAIN & PINE HILL STATION.

PUBLISCHT AND COPYRIGHTED BY H. SCHILE 19 & 16 DIVISION ST. N.Y.

SKETCHED FROM NATURE BY H. SCHILE

PANORAMA OF CATSKILL MOUNTAINS N.Y.

to leave the comforts of parlor or living room, guidebooks, picture books, maps, prints, and photographs have afforded vicarious opportunities to visit the Hudson Valley.

In 1822 Saratoga Springs printer and newspaper-editor Gideon Minor Davison published the first guidebook for America, *The Fashionable Tour; or, A trip to the Springs, Niagara, Quebeck, and Boston, in the Summer of 1821*, which took readers on a steamboat journey up the Hudson. Picture books further popularized Hudson River scenery, especially Nathanial Parker Willis's *American Scenery* (1840) and later William Cullen Bryant's *Picturesque America* (1872).

Between 1860 and 1920, the stereoscope became the most popular and far-reaching medium for bringing tourist sites into the home. The three-dimensional effect produced by the dual photographs offered entertainment and education, and—more than any other medium—created the illusion of being present at the sites.

Armchair tourism continues to thrive in the twenty-first century. With a keyboard and the click of a mouse, the Internet can take us anywhere and bring us images and sounds of tourist sites throughout the Hudson Valley.

(*this page*) TABLETOP STEREO VIEWER
Possibly England
Rosewood veneer on wood, glass, metal, ca. 1860–1870
u1981.8
Photography by Gary Gold

(*facing page*) PANORAMA OF CATSKILL MOUNTAINS
H. Schile
Colored lithograph on paper, ca. 1870
1997.9.2
Photography by Gary Gold

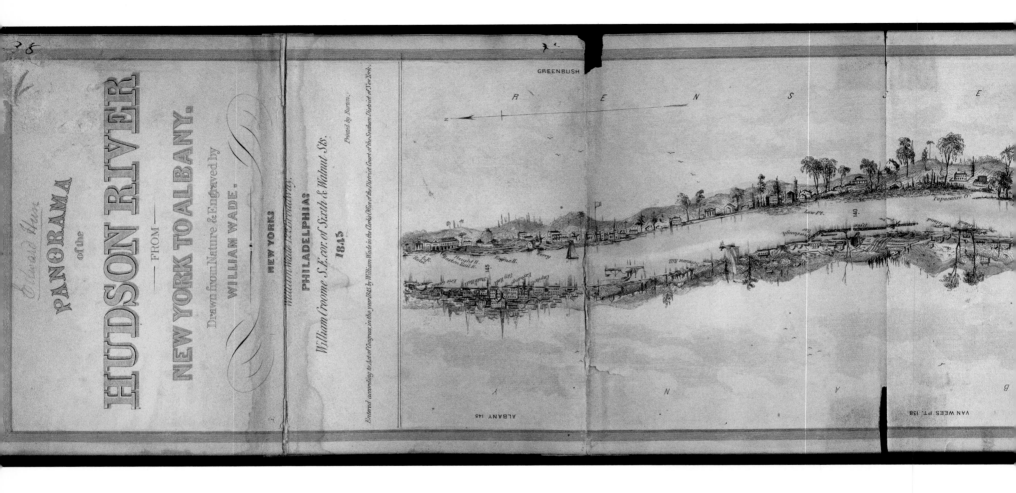

PANORAMA OF THE HUDSON RIVER (DETAIL)

Published by William Wade, New York City, and William Croome, Philadelphia
Colored engraving on paper, 1845
Library special collection

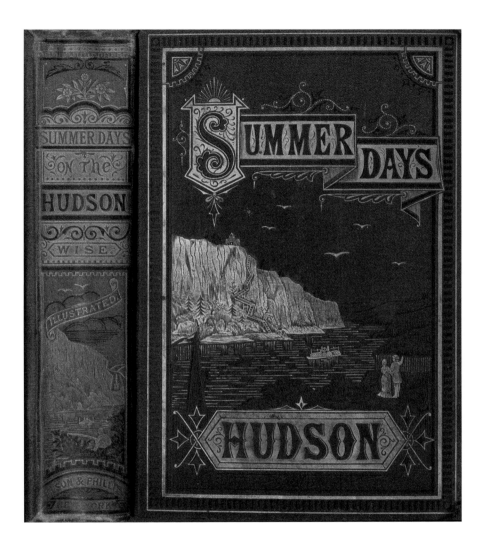

BINDING OF SUMMER DAYS ON THE HUDSON BY DANIEL WISE

Published by Nelson & Phillips, New York City
Gilt and ink stamped cloth over cardboard, 1875
Library special collection

ART AND NATURE AND
THE HUDSON RIVER SCHOOL

The Development of an American Landscape Movement
Throughout most of the seventeenth and eighteenth centuries, the American wilderness was portrayed as a dangerous, evil, and untamed place. Americans generally believed that the land and its resources were intended for food and shelter rather than for aesthetic enjoyment. Yet by the early nineteenth century, a radical change had occurred in the perception of the natural environment. For the first time, the untamed wilderness became a "landscape," a source of American pride viewed as a valuable cultural and economic resource.

Prior to 1825, portraiture, religious art, and historical scenes dominated as the main genres of painting, which demanded that both artist and audience have firm grounding in literature, history, and the classics. The rare landscape paintings executed during this time derived from the military tradition of topographical drawing.

American literature, influenced by European romanticism, figured prominently in bringing a change of opinion about the natural world. Prior to 1800, the main body of American writing focused on religion and politics. Beginning in 1819, however, three American writers, Washington Irving, James Fenimore Cooper, and William Cullen Bryant (often referred to as the "Knickerbockers"), stressed the uniqueness of America, with nature being the most popular subject.

The Hudson River School

Considered to be the first American school of painting, the Hudson River school consisted of two generations of artists working from the 1820s through the 1870s who painted primarily landscapes, especially large panoramic views of North and South America, Europe, and the Middle East. Their subject matter ranged from sublime views of the wilderness to beautiful, pastoral scenes to allegorical pictures with moral and even political messages.

The wilderness of the Hudson River valley and Catskill Mountains inspired English-born artist Thomas Cole, considered the founder of the informal school, to paint pictures of the American landscapes that captured the imagination. His distinctive landscape paintings helped to separate American culture from that of Europe at the same time that writers began extolling the beauty of the American landscape and equating God with nature. Other ingredients that helped to pave the way for the success of the Hudson River school included a reasonable transportation system, satisfactory overnight accommodations in the mountains, and guidebooks about how to enjoy the mountains. Furthermore, a stable government and growing economy helped to support art patronage and a rise in tourism.

The phrase "Hudson River School" was first used by a critic from the *New York Herald Tribune* in 1872 to describe the "old fashion style" of American landscape painting, as opposed to the new, more painterly and impressionistic style of the French Barbizon artists. Today many painters who work in a neo-romantic style continue to draw inspiration from the Hudson River school.

Thomas Cole and Asher B. Durand

Born in England but inspired by the wildness of the American landscape, the self-taught artist Thomas Cole developed a painting style based on a naturalistic yet romanticized view of nature. He sold his first paintings in 1825, considered the beginning of the Hudson River school. Common imagery in Cole's work includes cascading water, passing storm clouds with emerging sunlight, twisted and blasted tree trunks, and figures, such as in his view of Lake Winnipesaukee, completed from a series of sketches made while touring New Hampshire's White Mountains. His work speaks to the rebirth and regeneration of nature.

After Cole's death in 1848, Asher B. Durand became the leading figure of the second-generation Hudson River school artists. Distancing himself from Cole's romanticized landscape formula, Durand focused on a more literal transcription of nature. *Cathedral Ledge* exemplifies the accuracy of his work. Some years ago, a rock climber visiting the Albany Institute was studying a Durand painting referred to as *The Shawangunks* (1855) when he observed that the rock formations in the painting were vertical, like those found in the White Mountains of New Hampshire, rather than horizontal, like rocks found in the Shawangunks. Further research revealed that Durand was working in North Conway during the summer of 1855. Topographical comparison led curators to retitle the painting *Cathedral Ledge*, a known feature in the White Mountains.

(facing page) LAKE WINNIPESAUKEE
Thomas Cole (1801–1848)
Oil on canvas, 1827 or 1828
Gift of Dorothy Treat Arnold (Mrs. Ledyard Jr.) Cogswell, 1949.1.4
Photography by Joseph Levy

Journey into the Landscape

Hudson River school artists made numerous and sometimes arduous sketching trips to mountains, lakes, and exotic locations during the warmer months. They often traveled on foot, by small boat, or on horseback with paint boxes, small canvases, sketchbooks, and journals, along with portable stools, easels, and umbrellas. During the colder months, artists worked in their studios, often in New York City, painting, participating in exhibitions, meeting patrons, and selling their art. Painters frequently included color and atmospheric notations in their journals for future reference. A key technological improvement for artists was "collapsible, compressible metal [paint] tubes," invented in 1841 by John Rand. These new tubes held portable, premixed pigments that did not dry out. Prior to this innovation, artists often had to mix their own paints and store them in animal bladders, a messy and time-consuming task.

(*this page*) THE ARTIST (DETAIL)
William Richardson Tyler (1825–1896)
Oil on canvas, ca. 1870
u1977.389
Photography by Gary Gold

(*facing page*)
CATHEDRAL LEDGE

Asher B. Durand (1796–1886)
Oil on canvas, 1855
Gift of Jane E. Rosell, 1987.20.4
Photography by Joseph Levy

Frederic Edwin Church and Sanford Robinson Gifford

Frederic Edwin Church, another second-generation Hudson River school artist, excelled as a master of the panoramic landscape. He was also a gifted draftsman and a superb colorist. In 1844 he moved to Catskill, New York, and spent two years studying with Thomas Cole; he was one of only two artists to do so. In *Morning, Looking East over the Hudson Valley from the Catskill Mountains*, Church depicts the celebrated view from the Catskill escarpment looking east over the Hudson Valley, with the yellow and orange rays of the sun reflected in the Hudson River below. In 1860 Church bought farmland across the river in Hudson, New York, with a commanding view of both the river and the Catskill Mountains. Here he built a spectacular Persian-style villa he called "Olana," which in Arabic means "center of the world."

Sanford Robinson Gifford, an artist who hailed from Hudson, was a contemporary of Church noted for his mastery of the various effects of light. He traveled extensively through the eastern and western United States as well as throughout Europe and the Middle East. *Mount Merino and the City of Hudson in Autumn* is an early example of his work. The painting, based on a sketch made from Gifford's family property, overlooks the city from the north. Gifford typically progressed from pencil sketch to oil sketch and then from a medium- to large-sized canvas, depending on the patron's wishes.

Jasper Cropsey and George Inness

Jasper Cropsey is best known for his paintings depicting the vivid colors of the autumn landscape. The invention of synthetic aniline dyes in 1856, which made it possible for artists to record more accurate transcriptions of nature, was essential to his bright palette. When he painted *Dawn of Morning, Lake George* in 1868, Lake George was a well-traveled tourist destination, quite different from the unspoiled landscape depicted in his painting. In this romanticized view, Cropsey reflects upon the theme of change. A lone Native American sits on the bank of the wild but beautiful lake; however, a sailboat in the far distance, signaling the arrival of the white man, serves as a harbinger of change to this peaceful world.

First exhibiting his paintings in 1844, the prolific artist George Inness enjoyed a long career. While his early work reflected the spirit of the second-generation Hudson River school artists, by the 1860s he had moved away from the meticulous details advocated by Asher B. Durand and instead took inspiration from the more spontaneous, impressionistic, and soft-edged techniques of French Barbizon painters. In *An Adirondack Pastorale*, Inness relies on the play between atmospheric elements—hazy, light summer sky and the lush, dark-green woodlands of the Adirondacks.

(facing page)
MORNING, LOOKING EAST OVER THE HUDSON VALLEY FROM THE
CATSKILL MOUNTAINS

Frederic Edwin Church (1826–1900)
Oil on canvas, 1848
Gift of Catherine Gansevoort (Mrs. Abraham) Lansing
X1940.606.7
Photography by Joseph Levy

Dawn of Morning, Lake George

Jasper Cropsey (1823–1900)
Oil on canvas, 1868
1943.95
Photograph by Joseph Levy

An Adirondack Pastorale

George Inness (1825–1894)
Oil on canvas, 1869
Bequest of Marjorie Doyle Rockwell, 1995.30.2
Photography by Gary Gold

119

Neo-Hudson River School Painters

Artists today still turn to the American landscape for inspiration. Hudson Valley resident and painter Bill Sullivan depicts iconic landscapes of New York State, including stunning views of the Hudson River, Catskill Mountains, Niagara Falls, and New York City, as well as the volcanoes and waterfalls of Colombia, Ecuador, and Venezuela. Though he was grounded in the principles of Abstract Expressionism, Sullivan's first introduction to the work of Frederic Church changed his life: "I was conscious of a connection between the Abstract Expressionists who were the heroes of my youth, and the Hudson River school. They both represented a New World vision, and both sought an ambitious and heroic scale and monumentality that I wanted to make my own."

ANDREW JACKSON DOWNING
AND HUDSON RIVER ARCHITECTURE

The Picturesque Ideal

The Hudson River valley is an architecturally distinctive region representing more than four centuries of diverse building styles, ranging from elaborate mansions to modest farmhouses and working-class dwellings. In the mid-nineteenth century, Andrew Jackson Downing, a landscape architect and nurseryman from Newburgh,

New York, wrote a series of pattern books for home and garden plans. His ideas, which influenced the suburbanization of America, were originally inspired by the scenic beauty of the Hudson Valley, especially its picturesque qualities.

In architecture, the idea of the picturesque influenced the

ALBANY RURAL CEMETERY
William Hart (1823–1894), Albany
Oil on canvas in gilt frame, 1849
1948.22
Photography by Gary Gold

design and setting of buildings, which were composed as works of art. Downing's desire to create simple cottage dwellings that were accessible and could be enjoyed by all classes of society motivated a movement for community renewal. Architects responded with designs prompted by Romantic revivals of "natural" architecture, notably those following Gothic and Renaissance themes. A prolific writer, Downing popularized the new picturesque taste. Although he had few actual projects to his credit, his articles, books, and the

WASHINGTON PARK, ALBANY, NEW YORK
Unidentified photographer
Silver gelatin photographic print, ca. 1905
Morris Gerber photograph collection, 1993.10.10205P

periodical he founded, *The Horticulturist*, proved tremendously influential throughout the United States.

Public Spaces

Landscaped rural cemeteries, popular in the 1830s and 1840s, were the precursors and models for large public parks that began to be developed in the 1850s. As cities grew and churchyard burial grounds became inadequate and posed health concerns, city officials proposed alternative rural sites on the outskirts of town. Rural cemetery plans emphasized proximity to nature and—in keeping with the Romantic movement—were based on models in France, such as Père Lachaise Cemetery, and the great landscaped estates of England. These cemeteries became social meeting spaces for citizens, who could stroll or ride through the landscape and around the sculptural monuments.

123

(*this page*) RESIDENCE OF JAMES WAGER

Published by Harry Pease, Albany
Lithograph on paper, ca. 1860
Bequest of Ledyard Cogswell Jr., 1954.59.95

(*facing page*)
CORRESPONDENCE BETWEEN WM. P. VAN RENSSELAER AND A. J.
DOWNING, WITH VIEW OF DOWNING'S HOME, HIGHLAND GARDEN

Relief cut and ink on paper, ca. 1838
Manuscript collection, BM 400

Following the lead of Mount Auburn Cemetery in Cambridge, Massachusetts, and Greenwood Cemetery in Brooklyn, Major D. B. Douglass designed Albany Rural Cemetery in 1841, the same year that Andrew Jackson Downing published his treatise on the theory and practice of landscape gardening.

Highland Gardens
Newburgh Aug 9—

Dear Sir,

I have the
pleasure of forwarding you in a wrapper
a proof of my view of Beaverwyck
with the leaf of text which accompanies
it.
from my long delayed second edition of
the Landscape Gardening. There are many
beautiful new illustrations which I hope
with much new matter will render it
a much more valuable work.

Mrs Downing and I expect to be at

Mr Rathbones during the first part of
next week and I promise myself
the pleasure of examining some of
the many improvements which I
learn you have made since I
was last at your residence. Believe
me dear sir, with much respect

Your obed'ent servant

Wm P. Van Rensselaer Eq   A. J. Downing

DOLLHOUSE

Manufactured by Superior, Marx Co., Thomas Toys, and Plasco
Mixed materials, ca. 1954
Gift of Linda Bordwell, 2007.31
Photography by Gary Gold

In 1850, as a result of the reputation gained from his books, Downing was awarded a commission to develop the landscape plan for the National Mall in Washington, D.C. This formal design initiated a period of specialized attention to many public spaces.

Following Downing's death in 1852, Frederick Law Olmsted of Boston assumed leadership of the project. Olmsted planned parks, parkways, and suburbs throughout the nation such as Manhattan's Central Park, designed with Downing's protégé Calvert Vaux in 1858. Olmsted and Vaux also designed other parks in the region, including Washington Park in Albany and Downing Park in Newburgh.

The Birth of the Suburbs

Andrew Jackson Downing's promotion of the detached single-family house set within a planned landscape heralded the suburban movement in the United States. The growing middle class, able to afford these new houses, looked for opportunities to relocate outside cities but not necessarily to remote countryside. Transportation improvements, notably the railroad, made it possible for people to work in town and live in tastefully planned "natural" settings.

In 1850 Downing and his partner Alexander Jackson Davis published plans for an ideal "country village," with detached houses set on tree-lined streets surrounding a public park. Their publication, *The Architecture of Country Houses: Including Designs for Cottages, and Farm-Houses and Villas, With Remarks on Interiors, Furniture, and the Best Modes of Warming and Ventilating*, included detailed sections on ventilation and heating, interior layout, and furniture design. Like Downing's other works, it drew heavily on English prototypes.

The American Domestic Ideal

The idea of "home" in the mid-nineteenth century meant a comfortable dwelling decorated with furniture and possessions. Andrew Jackson Downing, and architects who followed, believed that to understand "home" as merely a fulfillment of the human need for shelter meant overlooking the place it held in the imagination and its powerful potential for cultural change. Beginning in the late nineteenth century, architect George F. Barber personalized plans for individual clients at moderate costs. William A. Radford, known for his artistic bungalows, twin and double houses, and apartment buildings, also published plan books between 1880 and 1930.

Perhaps the most revolutionary concept in home construction occurred when kit homes were first marketed by Aladdin Company and then by Sears Modern Homes in 1908, making it possible for families to purchase houses sooner than if they had to pay the costs of standard building practices.

What constitutes the ideal home today varies as widely as home styles themselves, and models, whether in the form of children's toys or popular magazines, still guide and influence our decisions.

UNTITLED (TROPHY)

Chester Rose
Oil on linen, 1989
1990.15.1
Photography by
Joseph Levy

Selected Bibliography

Avery, Kevin J., and Franklin Kelly, eds. *Hudson River School Visions: The Landscapes of Sanford R. Gifford.* New York: Metropolitan Museum of Art, 2003.

Blackburn, Roderic H., and Ruth Piwonka. *Remembrance of Patria: Dutch Arts and Culture in Colonial America, 1609–1776.* Albany: Albany Institute of History & Art, 1988.

Bradley, James W. *Before Albany: An Archaeology of Native-Dutch Relations in the Capital Region, 1600–1664.* Albany: New York State Deptartment of Education, 2007.

Bruegel, Martin. *Farm, Shop, Landing: The Rise of a Market Society in the Hudson Valley, 1780–1860.* Durham, NC: Duke University Press, 2002.

Buel, Jesse. *Jesse Buel, Agricultural Reformer: Selections from his Writings.* Edited by Harry J. Carmen. New York: Columbia University Press, 1947.

Cooper, Wendy. *Classical Taste in America, 1800–1840.* Baltimore: Baltimore Museum of Art, 1993.

Corbett, Theodore. *The Making of American Resorts: Saratoga Springs, Ballston Spa, Lake George.* New Brunswick, NJ: Rutgers University Press, 2001.

Deak, Gloria Gilda. *Picturing America, 1497–1899.* 2 vols. Princeton: Princeton University Press, 1988.

Diamant, Lincoln. *Chaining the Hudson: The Fight for the River in the American Revolution.* New York: Fordham University Press, 2004.

Dunwell, Frances F. *The Hudson: America's River.* New York: Columbia University Press, 2008.

Ferber, Linda S., ed. *Kindred Spirits: Asher B. Durand and the American Landscape.* New York: Brooklyn Museum, 2007.

Gassan, Richard H. *The Birth of American Tourism: New York, the Hudson Valley, and American Culture, 1790–1830.* Amherst: University of Massachusetts Press, 2008.

Groft, Tammis Kane. *Cast with Style: Nineteenth Century Cast-Iron Stoves from the Albany Area.* Rev. ed. Albany: Albany Institute of History & Art, 1984.

———. *The Folk Spirit of Albany.* Albany: Albany Institute of History & Art, 1978.

———, and Mary Alice Mackay, eds. *Albany Institute of History & Art: 200 Years of Collecting.* New York: Hudson Hills Press, 1998. In association with Albany Institute of History & Art.

Hendrick, Ulysses Prentiss. *A History of Agriculture in the State of New York.* New York: Hill and Wang, 1966.

Horrell, Jeffrey L. *Seneca Ray Stoddard: Transforming the Adirondack Wilderness in Text and Image.* Syracuse: Syracuse University Press, 1999.

Howard, David Sanctuary, and Conrad Edick Wright. *New York and the China Trade.* New York: New-York Historical Society, 1984.

Howat, John K. *Frederic Church.* New Haven: Yale University Press, 2005.

———. *American Paradise: The World of the Hudson River School.* New York: Metropolitan Museum of Art, 1987.

Hutton, George V. *The Great Hudson River Brick Industry: Commemorating Three and a Half Centuries of Brickmaking.* Fleischmanns, NY: Purple Mountain Press, 2003.

Johnson, Kathleen Eagen. *The Hudson-Fulton Celebration: New York's River Festival of 1909 and the Making of a Metropolis.* New York: Fordham University Press, 2009.

Lewis, Tom. *The Hudson: A History.* New Haven: Yale University Press, 2005.

Major, Judith K. *To Live in the New World: A. J. Downing and American Landscape Gardening.* Cambridge: MIT Press, 1997.

Marling, Karal Ann. *George Washington Slept Here: Colonial Revivals and American Culture, 1876–1986.* Cambridge: Harvard University Press, 1988.

Myers, Kenneth. *The Catskills: Painters, Writers, and Tourists in the Mountains, 1820–1895.* Yonkers, NY: Hudson River Museum of Westchester, 1987.

Nash, Roderick. *Wilderness and the American Mind.* 3rd ed. New Haven: Yale University Press, 1982.

Novak, Barbara. *Nature and Culture: American Landscape and Painting, 1825–1875*. New York: Oxford University Press, 1980.

Oleson, Alexandra, and Sanforn C. Brown, eds. *The Pursuit of Knowledge in the Early American Republic: American Scientific and Learned Societies from Colonial Times to the Civil War*. Baltimore: Johns Hopkins University Press, 1976.

Parry, Ellwood C. *The Art of Thomas Cole: Ambition and Imagination*. Newark: University of Delaware Press, 1988.

Philip, Cynthia Owen. *Robert Fulton: A Biography*. New York: Franklin Watts, 1985.

Phillips, Ruth B. *Trading Identities: The Souvenir in Native North American Art from the Northeast, 1700–1900*. Seattle: University of Washington Press, 1998.

Schullery, Paul. *American Fly Fishing: A History*. New York: Nick Lyons Books, 1987.

Schuyler, David. *Apostle of Taste: Andrew Jackson Downing, 1815–1852*. Baltimore: Johns Hopkins University Press, 1996.

Sears, John F. *Sacred Places: American Tourist Attractions in the Nineteenth Century*. New York: Oxford University Press, 1989.

Sheriff, Carol. *The Artificial River: The Erie Canal and the Paradox of Progress, 1817–1862*. New York: Hill and Wang, 1997.

Shorto, Russell. *The Island at the Center of the World: The Epic Story of Dutch Manhattan and the Forgotten Colony that Shaped America*. New York: Doubleday, 2004.

Sigur, Hannah. *The Influence of Japanese Art on Design*. Layton, UT: Gibbs Smith, 2008.

Stevens, Frank Walker. *The Beginnings of the New York Central Railroad: A History*. New York: G. P. Putnam's Sons, 1926.

Stilgoe, John R. *Borderland: Origins of the American Suburb, 1820–1939*. New Haven: Yale University Press, 1988.

Stradling, David. *Making Mountains: New York City and the Catskills*. Seattle: University of Washington Press, 2008.

Terrie, Philip G. *Contested Terrain: A New History of Nature and People in the Adirondacks*. Blue Mountain Lake, NY: Adirondack Museum, 1997.

Van Zandt, Roland. *The Catskill Mountain House*. New Brunswick, NJ: Rutgers University Press, 1966.

Venema, Janny. *Beverwyck: A Dutch Village on the American Frontier, 1652–1664*. Albany: State University of New York Press, 2003.

Webb, Nina H. *Footsteps through the Adirondacks: The Verplanck Colvin Story*. Utica, NY: North Country Books, 1996.

Wilcoxen, Charlotte. *Dutch Trade and Ceramics in America in the Seventeenth Century*. Albany: Albany Institute of History & Art, 1987.

Zimmerman, Karl. *20th Century Limited*. St. Paul: MBI, 2002.

Index